For Jack Kingsbury and the
Shoals Lab, whose operations
would make Cedric very happy.
All good wishes for the years ahead.
                    Fred McGill Jr.
July 21, 1974

Number 196
*of an edition
limited to 1000 copies*

LETTERS TO CELIA

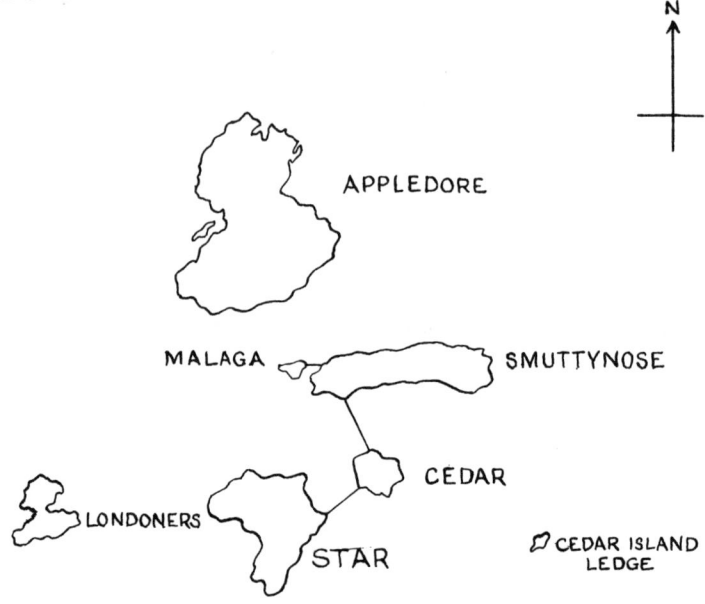

LETTERS TO CELIA

*Written during the years 1860-1875
to Celia Laighton Thaxter by her brother*
CEDRIC LAIGHTON

Edited with Notes and Drawings by
Frederick T. McGill, Jr.

Frederick T. McGill, Jr.

The Star Island Corporation
Boston · Massachusetts · 1972

© 1972 The Star Island Corporation

Designed by Burton L. Stratton

Printed and bound in the United States of America under the direction of
Publishing Services
Yarmouth Port, Massachusetts 02675

ACKNOWLEDGMENTS

I hope that the many helpful ones who have contributed in their several ways to this edition are aware of my gratitude, as I cannot mention all of them by name. I must, however, single out Mr. and Mrs. Edward A. Dodd of North Hampton, New Hampshire, Mr. Lawrence R. Craig of Portsmouth, Miss Dorothy Vaughan of the Portsmouth Public Library, Mr. Malcolm M. Ferguson of Concord, Massachusetts, and Miss Rosamond Thaxter of Kittery Point, Maine—all of whom gave me substantial assistance.

In addition, there are three persons whose contributions have been absolutely essential.

The first transcription of Cedric Laighton's letters to his sister—perhaps three times the length of the present text—was done several years ago by Miss Anne Forbes, Mr. Laighton's granddaughter. Although my own edition is taken from the original letters, I was helped immeasurably in the selection process by having the entire correspondence before me in typewritten form.

Throughout the fifty years that I have known the Isles of Shoals, my chief guide into the mysteries of the islands has been Lyman V. Rutledge, historian, watcher of sunrises, and friend. Recently I have leaned heavily on his knowledge and judgment in preparing my footnotes.

Most of all, I thank Cedric Laighton's daughter, Mrs. William B. Durant (Barbara Laighton), the owner of the letters, for permission to publish them, for the sharing of her recollections, and for encouragement along the way.

Frederick T. McGill, Jr.
Short Hills, New Jersey

FOREWORD

In the late eighteen-hundreds, almost everyone in New England had heard of the Isles of Shoals. Some knew the islands as a popular summer resort, serving upwards of six hundred guests at its two hotels. Others knew the islands through the writings of Celia Thaxter, who had transmuted into verse and singing prose the experiences of girlhood and womanhood on those historic rocks. The thousands who visited the Isles in the course of a summer knew that the hotels and Mrs. Thaxter were inseparable; that her father had built the Appledore House, that her brothers, Oscar and Cedric Laighton, were the proprietors of both inns, and that she herself presided over a Yankee version of the *salon*. Hundreds of lucky guests had been invited into Mrs. Thaxter's cottage parlor, where framed engravings of the Old Masters and of foreign scenes combined with the oils and water colors of the modern impressionists. In that hospitable room some had heard John Knowles Paine play Chopin on the grand piano, or John Greenleaf Whittier read his latest ballad. It was a shrine where Beauty was worshiped in her many forms.

In all the arts, this was the sunset hour of romanticism. This final quarter-century at Appledore glows across the years as a charming period piece, under that flaming western sky which lights so many of Mrs. Thaxter's poems.

It is we, however, who create this nostalgic tableau. The men and women who decorate the picture were in real life no more static than ourselves. Even Celia had already defied classification by producing a series of local color sketches that would later be labeled "realism." Her brothers were men of differing but exceptional talent who shared with her the risks and the rewards of Appledore's Golden Age. One of my hopes in presenting these letters of Cedric is that they will add vitality to our understanding of that period by giving us an intimate acquaintance with those people and events mainly responsible for shaping it. Instead of looking back on a glorious age that has passed, we shall become contemporary with the writer of these letters, and shall look forward with him as he and Oscar develop the family enterprise.

The correspondence offered in this volume runs from 1860 to 1875. Those unfamiliar with the Laighton story may be helped by a few paragraphs about the chain of events that antedate these letters.

Early in October, 1839, Thomas B. Laighton sailed from Portsmouth, New Hampshire, to the Isles of Shoals. With him were his wife, Eliza, and his two little children. Celia was four years old, Oscar three months. As the little ship set her course toward the southeast, none of the four realized to what degree their lives also were pointing in a new direction.

Laighton had made some specific plans for the immediate future, and no doubt his wife had shared in the decisions. He had accepted a two-year term as keeper of the lighthouse at White Island, a lonely outpost some eight miles off the coast. What made this move a puzzle to his associates was Laighton's standing as a prominent citizen of New Hampshire. He was a successful business man in Portsmouth and a member of the State Senate, already in his second term. But as he packed his family and his goods for the White Island adventure, he kept mum and let the curious ones guess about his motives.

The Isles of Shoals are nine points of rock which puncture the Atlantic just off the shores of Rye. A thin coating of sod allows grass and shrubs to flourish, along with a great variety of blossoming plants, giving color and fragrance to the summer landscape. But there are almost no trees, and there is nothing to break the winds of winter except the higher ledges of granite and the simple houses that men have raised to make existence possible.

Before Thomas Laighton took on his lighthouse assignment, he had already purchased four of the nine islands: Hog, Malaga, Smuttynose, and Cedar, in the hope that he could bring back the fishing industry to its early pre-eminence. The government owned White, where the lighthouse stood, and Seavey's, connected to White by a narrow isthmus at low tide. Star Island carried on its back the tiny village of Gosport, with possibly one hundred residents where several times that number had flourished as fishermen and merchants in colonial days. Two other small islands, Londoners and Duck, were uninhabited.

Probably Laighton expected to make an early return to mainland life. He appears to have been biding his time until he could move into the Postmastership in Portsmouth, which had been promised him. In the meantime the lighthouse job would allow him to work at revitalizing the fishing industry at the Shoals. Yet during his first four years at the islands he traveled continually back and forth. He finished out his Senate term, accepted two more years in the lower House, and performed minor political assignments in Portsmouth. Only when he learned in 1843 that the Postmastership had been awarded to a rival did he turn his full attention to the islands. After that date he never set foot on the mainland.

Meanwhile his children were happy and healthy in their new surroundings. In September of 1840 one more child was born, the boy they christened Cedric, and the family was now complete. Their mother radiated warmth and affection to all around her, and the credit must go to her above all for the secure and merry spirits of her little family. Long afterwards, when Celia told the story of those memorable years, she said: "I do not think a happier triad ever existed than we were, living in that profound isolation."

Despite his many other activities, Laighton found time to teach his children the three R's—with remarkable success, as the future was to prove. For a year or two when his duties on the mainland were most demanding, he moved his family to Smuttynose Island, and his brother-in-law, Joseph Cheever, operated the light. Otherwise they lived on White until the fall of 1847.

After 1846, however, the rebirth of the fishing industry became one of Laighton's lesser concerns. Henceforth he worked to develop a summer resort for mainlanders seeking health and recreation. That year he remade an old building on Smuttynose and opened it to the public as the Mid Ocean House, with a bowling alley as a special attraction. The response was immediate. Among the guests in 1846 were Franklin Pierce, than a United States Senator; Nathaniel Hawthorne; Governor John Page; Levi Woodbury; and Caleb Cushing. Other guests, less distinguished, were equally helpful in providing dollars and cents. The enterprise was promising.

For several years Laighton had dreamed of building a substantial hotel on Hog Island, and the dream at last was realized through a partnership with Levi Lincoln Thaxter, a young man who had been casting about for a vocation. Thaxter's father, a wealthy banker in Watertown, Massachusetts, had put his son through Harvard College and Harvard Law School, eager to see him established in a lucrative profession; but the younger Thaxter had leaned more toward the stage, and had even taken elocution lessons with Charles Kean, the actor. In the summer of 1846, still uncertain about a career, he had visited the Shoals for almost a month, striking up a warm friendship with the Laightons. The beauty of the islands and the apparent prosperity of the Mid Ocean House persuaded him that dozens of his young friends would follow him out there if the accommodations were available. It occurred to him that perhaps he might promote this development. Another year and another long visit later, Thaxter had determined his course and convinced his father that here was a good investment of life and capital. At the end of the summer— September, 1847—the senior Thaxter paid Laighton $2500 for one-half of Hog Island, and that same month Thomas Laighton and Levi Thaxter went into partnership to erect a "public house" on the island.

Hog now became Appledore, a name applied in the seventeenth century to the township embracing all the islands. The men went to work on their new building immediately, and were able to open the Appledore House to the public on June 15, 1848.

The first season was a "fair success," but Thaxter had decided by the end of summer that he was not cut out to be an innkeeper. Apparently there was too much menial labor for his taste, and his senior partner relegated to him too many of the disagreeable chores. Yet Thaxter had become almost a member of the family, and especially a favorite of the children, whom he had been tutoring. Therefore he made only a partial break. He and Laighton agreed that the partnership should be dissolved, but that he should retain the North Cottage, which had been his home for the past year.

There was a further problem. Levi discovered that he was in love with Celia, and although she was only thirteen at the time, asked her father in the conventional manner for her hand. The answer appears to have been a resounding "No!" but Thaxter determined to keep his residence on the island and lay siege, trusting that time would work in his favor. And so it proved to be. Sometime before Celia's fifteenth birthday, her father gave his reluctant consent to the marriage, provided it be postponed for at least a year. In the winter of 1849-50 Celia had her one experience with formal schooling. She attended the Mount Washington Female Seminary in South Boston, which allowed her a closer acquaintance with the Thaxters and their friends. Levi's father was even less happy about the match than Thomas Laighton, but he also relented, and "Levi's mermaid" won the family over with her simplicity and frankness.

They were married in the "south parlor" of the Appledore House on September 30, 1851. The Reverend John Weiss shared in the ceremony—one of Thaxter's classmates and closest friends, the minister of the Unitarian church in New Bedford. Oscar recalled many years later that "At the wedding-dinner, Weiss and Thaxter were doing their best to make mother laugh, for she seemed near tears. These young men were as fond of her as they would have been were she their own mother."

For several years after their marriage, the young Thaxters moved frequently, as Levi continued his search for a vocation. During the summers they were usually at Appledore, dividing their attention between the private life of their cottage and the society of the hotel. Their first child, Karl, was born at Appledore in July of 1852, their second, John, in November of 1854 at Curzon's Mill near Newburyport, another of their temporary homes. The Curzon family, owners of an old grist mill and a substantial residence, had been taking boarders for more than twenty years; and one of the daughters, Mrs. Elizabeth Hoxie, had become Celia's intimate friend. At times also the Thaxters stayed with Levi's parents in Watertown. Of these early years, the most memorable began in the spring of 1853, when Levi and a young clergyman were called to serve jointly as "missionaries" to the village of Gosport on Star Island, and the Thaxters were given the parsonage as their home. Celia reveled in this year-round closeness to every person and every thing she held most dear, and in the opportunity to serve the neighbors she had known so long.

These wanderings ended in 1856. In that year the Thaxters settled down in Newtonville, Massachusetts, in a large house bought for them by Levi's father. Across a broad field they could see the sparkling waters of the Charles River. Celia liked the house and its nearness to the river, but longed to travel with the current down to the open ocean.

Enough of this chronicle. The letters will carry on the story. But regarding the correspondence a few more remarks are in order.[1]

We cannot expect to learn much from these pages about the happy confusion of midsummer on the broad piazza of the Appledore House, or the conversations of writers, painters, and musicians in Celia's parlor, for at such times Celia had no need of letters from her brothers. Nor will there be more than hints of her growing stature as a public figure, after her reputation as a poet was established in the 1860's. What the letters give us is a compelling serial story of a family whose lives and whose love for one another have been built upon a rock; whose joys spring from the simplest delights: the glint of ice crystals, the season's first song sparrow, a steaming fish chowder, a play on words, a schooner under full sail, a letter from the mainland, a bit of finished handcraft from the shop or the sewing room. In the background is that wider island world of Gosport, across the

---

[1]. No editorial changes have been made in the original letters except for occasional alterations in spelling, punctuation, and indentation for the purposes of consistency and clarity.

"roads," with its hilarious comedy of Beebes and Caswells, interrupted by the tragic visitations of drowning and disease.

The reader who turns from these letters to the writings of Celia herself will find that her poetry and prose have taken on a new validity. In these days of loosening family ties, it is easy to charge the Victorians with hypocrisy, and to assume that any claim they made to domestic happiness was merely a public pose. Cedric's letters are convincing evidence that at least among the Laightons the ties of affection were tough and resilient, and that in stating her love Celia was not merely taking the line that current fashion demanded. Thus in her poetry what might seem sentimentality is often revealed as the purest sentiment. As for her prose masterpiece, *Among the Isles of Shoals*, it weaves into a balanced blend the same kinds of raw material that tumble haphazardly from Cedric's letters: the northeasters, the snowy owls, the shipwrecks, the uncouth and pathetic villagers, and all the rest. Our glimpses of that life as observed from day to day give a new appreciation of her skill in ordering and unifying the island story, in which the earthiness of Gosport village is one with the grandeur of the hurricane.

Perhaps the ultimate charm of this correspondence is something implicit: the writer's knowledge that she who receives the letters will feel about the events as the writer has felt; and there is a communication of spirit accented by the private nicknames and private jokes but essentially unspoken because it is unspeakable.

LETTERS
TO
CELIA

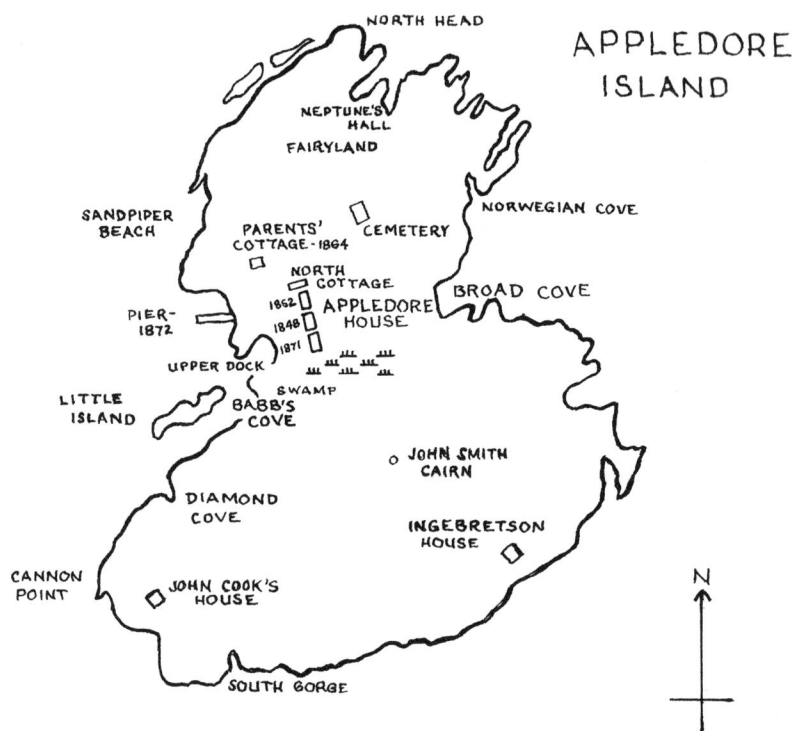

*   *   *January 1, 1860*   *   *

Dear Sister,

 I hasten to write to you, to let you know the proceedings at Appledore within the past week. We have had very cold weather here; Wednesday and Thursday last the glass stood at zero. Friday the wind which had been northwest hauled to the northeast, and the snow fell in clouds, effectually obscuring the view.

 During this storm a large brig from Havana bound to Portland was in where our moorings were last summer, thinking to get a harbor. The Captain soon discovered his error and endeavored to put the brig about but she being light missed stays and fell off in the wrong direction, and was driven plump onto the point of Babb's Cove,[1] close to Diamond Cove.[2] The first intimation we had of the fact was by the way of John Cook,[3] who came rushing into the kitchen escorting the Captain, who came to leave his chronometer in a place of safety. The Captain stated that he saw smooth water and ran in for a harbor. Every exertion was made to get her off, but all failed and every sea that came washed her up higher, dashing her on the rocks with great violence. At low water they ascertained that she was injured beyond repairing. Some of the Islanders are now engaged in taking the sails and rigging from the masts. The Captain and some of the men have gone home, and the others at Star Island are waiting for a chance to go to Portsmouth.

 Tell the dear children that we wish them a very merry New Year. Dominy[4] desires you to give them a good hug all round on her account.

 With much love to all, I remain, your
        Affectionate brother
        Cedy

 1. Babb's Cove: The most sheltered inlet on Appledore's west coast, protected on the north by Little Island (now commonly Babb's Rock). Philip Babb, for whom the cove and rock were named, was a seventeenth-century butcher and tavern keeper. His ghost appears in Shoals lore.
 2. Diamond Cove: Apparently what is now called Pepperell's Cove, near the southwest point of Appledore.
 3. John Cook: John Cook Randall, a fisherman celebrated for his

profanity, who lived in a cottage built for him by Levi Thaxter on the southwest point of Appledore.

4. Dominy: Sometimes shortened to "Dom," this was the grandchildren's name for Eliza Laighton, Cedric's mother.

* * *January 15, 1860* * *

Dear Sister,

I write you today to let you know that we are all enjoying health and happiness in an eminent degree, though the weather is certainly enough to drive anybody distracted. Nothing but one continual round of snowstorms; even now the snow is falling covering deeper and deeper the few shrubs which adorn the island. The sheep are in despair, and are huddled together looking mournfully at the falling snow, and the cows are tossing their heads in the wildest despair.

The brig now lays a shattered wreck—the masts, windlass and everything valuable has been taken ashore. The owner, Mr. Dyer of Portland, came down and stopped with us a few days. He said that there was a great quantity of copper in the vessel, so on Friday last they set fire to her to obtain it, and in the evening she was enveloped in flames, making a fine show. Showers of sparks were continually flying through the air, and many of them were driven by the strong southwest wind entirely over the house, and went

sailing down to Broad Cove.[1] We were somewhat alarmed lest the house should catch fire, and so we kept watch in the south parlor, till the rising tide nearly extinguished the flames, when we retired exceedingly sleepy.

With loads of love from all to all, I am, dear sister,

Your affectionate brother
Cedy

---

1. Broad Cove: This indentation on Appledore's eastern shore combines with Babb's Cove on the west side to give the island its "wasp waist."

* * *January 22, 1860* * *

Dear Sister,

Everything reminds me of you today. The ocean is swept by a gentle north wind; as I write I can look from the window down to Broad Cove, where we have gathered sea mosses and Irish moss so many times together. Four or five miles from the shore a Portland steamer is passing. I think of the journeys we used to take over the rough rocks about Norwegian Cove[1] in search of mosses, and how you used to reach down into deep ponds at the risk of tumbling in yourself, after precious specimens of green moss. I think of the wonderful fairy land, over at Neptune's Hall,[2] where we used to imagine we saw magic rings drawn in the grass, where the fairies used to dance and sing, as we thought. When I go over there I can still see the walls of that little house you built so many years ago. . . .

As the boat is about to start for Portsmouth, I shall have to end my letter here, so goodbye, dearest sister, and take the undying love of

Cedy

---

1. Norwegian Cove: A small dent in Appledore's eastern shore, just north of Broad Cove.
2. Neptune's Hall: A valley reaches in a southwesterly direction from the rugged north shore to Sandpiper Beach on the west side. In this valley was the area that the Laighton children called Fairyland. Neptune's Hall seems to have been one of the ravines at the northeastern end of this playground.

* * *February 5, 1860* * *

Dear Sister,

It is overcast today. Great black masses of clouds overhang the eastern sky, which indicates that we are about to have another snowstorm. February was ushered in by a howling northeaster; the mercury from 40 fell to 3 and the cold was more keenly felt from so sudden a change. The old brig rolls heavily to and fro with the motion of the sea, and mimic waterfalls may be seen rushing through the spike holes in her sides. I often think what a contrast she presents to the noble looking vessel she was when she first struck the point. The masts and spars still lie in Babb's Cove, where they were taken weeks ago. The recent storm has bruised them considerably, and if the owner don't send for them soon, he will find them pretty well chawed up.

This morning I took a row over to Star Island, and as I rowed along with the pleasant sound of water rippling along the boat's sides for company I thought to myself, I wish Sister was here that she might take a row too. Do you remember our unsuccessful fishing expedition last spring? I can't think why we were so unlucky. After you went away the fish were as thick as hops, and the way I hauled in big codfish was a caution.

Begging, dear Sister, that you will excuse my writing so much about the weather (which I assure you is the only item of importance with us) I will close, with heaps of love to all.

Yours affectionately,
Cedy

* * *February 12, 1860* * *

Dear Sister,

Your letter dated February second I received last Sunday, just after I sent my last letter, so I thought I would wait till today before answering it, that I might tell you all the news. Friday the wind came off to the northwest, and for twenty-four hours it blew a perfect hurricane. The spray dashed upon the Island in clouds, and in a short time the Little Island[1] was completely enveloped in ice, while the old brig was hurled by the powerful waves far up in Diamond Cove. We received papers yesterday in which it was stated that much damage was done in New York. Vessels sank in the harbor, buildings smashed, etc.

Mother's parrot performs wonders in the art of talking, and Bocky[2] declares that she converses freely on most every topic. She occasionally takes it into her head to fly onto Mother's flowers, causing them to bend and break in every direction.

Last Thursday an agent came from Portland after the rigging and masts, and for a while Babb's Cove was a scene of great activity and excitement. Small boats filled the cove, and the cry of the men as they hauled up the anchor could be heard for miles around.

Bocky says he shall write to Karly[3] today. Hoping, dear Sister, this will find you well and happy, I remain ever affectionately your

Brother Cedy

1. Little Island: Babb's Rock, the north wall of Babb's Cove.
2. Bocky: The family nickname for Oscar, Cedric's older brother.
3. Karly: Karl was Celia's oldest son, born July 24, 1852.

* * *May 27, 1860* * *

Dear Sister,

I received your welcome letter of the eighteenth, last Thursday, and we were all very glad to hear from you. I am perfectly delighted with the little poem[1] you so kindly sent me, and I shall keep it as long as I live, as a sad memorial of departed days, as Bocky would say. The dioletia is in full bloom, and is certainly a very beautiful little plant. Mother is delighted with it—the flowers are heart shaped, and hang down from the branches very prettily—the color is pink, with a little transparent edging of green at the top.

As the steamboat arrangement has failed, I suppose the *Sibyl*[2] will run, and I believe Father has already engaged Mr. Preble, who runs her, you know, though a steamboat would be a great convenience on account of the regularity of its trips. A sailboat will bring about as many as the house will accommodate, and, as you say, make it much easier. . . .

It certainly has been very dry for the season and we were forced to bring water from the ponds by Norwegian Cove previous to the showers of the nineteenth—many of the seeds have failed to come up in consequence of the drought. . . .

I wish that I could find something to write about that I might cover the sheet as you do, you dear, but as I cannot, I will subscribe myself most affectionately

Your brother,
Cedy

1. the little poem: Probably this was "Land-locked," which was destined to appear in the *Atlantic* for March, 1861. The success of this poem launched Celia on her literary career, and she always placed it first in all collections of her poems. See p. 26 for an account of its reception in print at Appledore. The first two stanzas, printed below, set the theme of homesickness:

> Black lie the hills; swiftly doth daylight flee;
>   And catching gleams of sunset's dying smile,
>   Through the dusk land for many a changing mile
> The river runneth softly to the sea.
>
> O happy river, could I follow thee!
>   O yearning heart that never can be still!
>   O wistful eyes that watch the steadfast hill,
> Longing for level line of solemn sea! . . .

2. *Sibyl*: This large and fast yacht did indeed run, as reported in the Portsmouth *Chronicle* of July 21, 1860: "The Hotels, both Appledore and Atlantic Houses, have . . . been much enlarged, improved and beautified; the yacht *Sibyl* runs to the Appledore, and the *Golden Eagle* to the Atlantic, from Portsmouth." The Atlantic House on Star Island was a modest competitor of the Appledore.

Captain Rufus Preble of the *Sibyl* was not one to give something for nothing. On what was apparently the final day of their 1860 contract, Thomas Laighton wrote the following in the hotel register:

> Sept. 20, 1860. The *Sibyl* did not come out—the Capt. being determined to ascertain the meaning of *"Inclusive."* Having satisfied himself upon this point he came out the 21st.

* * * November 18, 1860 * *

Dearest Sister,

Your long pleasant letter was received a short time since. We have been busy building a new workshop, as Father has written you, I believe. It is twenty-five feet long by twenty wide, and is quite a nice shop, I assure you. Mr. Folsom[1] arrived here last Tuesday; the poor fellow was detained in Portsmouth four days, and was delighted to behold the Island once more. He said several times, as I rowed him up to the wharf, "This is too good to be here again," and when we landed he said, "I could fall upon the earth and kiss it as Brutus did." This morning we went down all around the western shore after things to put in the aquarium, which is progressing finely. Starfish, urchins, whelks, clams, mussels, and all sorts of things animate and inanimate have been collected with great rapidity and skill. We have painted our little boat, and fixed a new sail for her, so she looks quite respectable. We hoisted the old sail the other day, intending to sail to Smutty,[2] when lo the bolt-rope parted on top, and our sail became instantly among the things that are not.

Mr. Manley[3] is an excellent young gentleman whom Dr. Bowditch[4] sent here to breathe this revivifying air, which you know is a sure cure for all lung diseases.

You shouldn't say that Karly[5] is disagreeable. I think he is quite an interesting little boy, and though he is rather plain looking now, I have no doubt he will change as he grows older. Most homely children grow up to be handsome men and women, to my way of thinking. Johnny's[6] shadow on the wall is perfect, and Mother is delighted with it. Yours, I think, does not resemble you much, because it is not half so pretty as you are.

Father is quite sick, having taken a violent cold somehow or other. It is too bad he should have to suffer anything but his lameness—isn't it? I pity him so much. Bocky says he will write soon.

Affectionately,
Cedy

1. Mr. Folsom: George M. Folsom of Cambridge was an intimate friend of

both the Laightons and the Thaxters. He had already visited Appledore twice this year, in July and August.

2. Smutty: Smuttynose, or Haley's Island, to the southeast of Appledore.

3. Mr. Manley: Sidney Manley became a devoted friend of the Laightons. He is frequently referred to in later years as "Partner."

4. Dr. Bowditch: Henry Ingersoll Bowditch, M.D., son of Nathaniel Bowditch of Salem, the authority on navigation. Dr. Henry Bowditch practiced in Boston.

5. Karly is disagreeable: From babyhood Karl showed signs of abnormality, and as he grew older he was increasingly unable to keep up with his brothers, either physically or mentally. See note, p. 134.

6. Johnny's: Celia's second son, John, was born November 29, 1854.

* * *December 2, 1860* * *

Dearest Sister,

Your kind letter arrived yesterday. Johnson[1] goes to Portsmouth once or twice every week, so you see our communication with the mainland is excellent.

The aquarium has not been turned upside down *once*, as yet, though the water has been changed several times, and fresh air is pumped in every now and then. Among the creatures Mr. Folsom has collected are a small sculpin and six little minnows, or rather three minnows, for the other half of them have been devoured by some rapacious inhabitant of the aquarium. Mr. Folsom suspects the sculpin of the dastardly deed.

The workshop is all finished and Bocky is perfectly happy. I suppose you know that he has erected a chimney in the building and has a little forge, making a blacksmith's shop and joiner's shop in one. A man came over from Smutty the other day, and asked him to make some irons to go on the bow and stern of a wherry, which he did with great skill, and to the entire satisfaction of the purchaser.

Old Lem[2] is still alive, though he cut his throat from ear to ear. He said he had been thinking about it for seven years. Isn't that horrible? How did you pass Thanksgiving Day? We enjoyed ourselves, and had a most magnificent dinner of roast turkey and plum pudding, not to mention two bottles of claret.. . . .

Mother is delighted with the scarf, and says it is worked beautifully. We have hung the shadows up in the dining room, and can see them every time we pass through. Mother thinks everything of them. Under Mr. Folsom's tuition, Polly is learning new words and sentences very fast, and says, "How are you, Polly, hey?" as plain as can be. . . .

Mother and Father send loads of love, and Bocky joins me with wishes for your everlasting happiness and health.

Yours affectionately,
Cedy

    1. Johnson: Christian Johnson, a fisherman, lived with his family on Star Island at this time, but later moved across the harbor to the "Red House" on Smuttynose. There he was a tenant of the Laightons, since Thomas Laighton had bought that island in 1839. Norwegian in origin, he probably spelled his name "Jansen," one of the several variant spellings in Cedric's letters.

    2. Lemuel Caswell, born November 1, 1796, a brother of Joseph M. Caswell, who kept the first known boarding house on Star Island, and an uncle of Lemuel B. Caswell, owner of the Atlantic House. "Old Lem" survived this suicide attempt but was successful in a second try the next year.

*   *   *December 6, 1860*   *   *

Dearest Sister,

    . . . Last Monday Mr. Remick came out to move the bowling alley. We have taken the alleys out of the main building and have made every preparation for moving. Today we moved the fish-house or bathing house from its old position in a direct line toward the yellow gate, and halted where the old fish-flake used to stand. Tomorrow we shall commence to move the old bowling alley itself. . . .

Bocky is out in his workshop tonight with Mr. Remick trying the forge. Mr. Folsom is sitting close by (I am writing in the parlor), writing with great rapidity. The sea-gulls seem to know that I want their wings,[1] for they never come within shot. Perhaps they saw my new gun when it was coming from Portsmouth. I shot a wild goose the other day.

Hoping this letter will give you half the pleasure yours did me, I am ever

Affectionately,
Cedy

    1. I want their wings: At this period Celia was eager for birds' wings to ornament her hats, and Cedric sent her the best specimens he could obtain.

Years later she was revolted by the thought of killing in order to feed woman's vanity, and she joined the Audubon Society, supporting its efforts to prevent the destruction of birds in the name of fashion.

* *   *December 9, 1860*   * *

Dear Sister,

. . . We got a package of mail today and Father got a letter from Mr. Manley, who is coming back again, and will probably be here Tuesday or Wednesday. Mr. Folsom is splitting wood today. He has collected quite a pile of drift wood, and seems to derive much amusement from the occupation. The process of moving the bowling alley progresses slowly. The old part which used to be a blacksmith shop is swung and pointed to its future resting place, which is to be up by the barn, you know, in that little hollow, between the hill and the barn.

It is a most beautiful day; there is scarcely any wind and the ocean is quite calm. I can see Mr. Folsom and Bocky skating down in the swamp, and though the space is small, they seem to be enjoying themselves at a great rate. Last evening we cracked a quantity of nuts, and sat up till a late hour of the night devouring them. Father has purchased four barrels of apples, and a barrel of walnuts, so you see we have all the elements of perfect happiness at hand.

As the mail bag is about to be closed, I will end my letter here, with love for all.

Ever affectionately,
Cedy

* *   *January 1, 1861*   * *

Oh, you dear Sister, four letters from you and none of them answered. I wonder at your patience. Now the bowling alley is moved I hope to be more punctual in answering your letters. How you ever contrive to write such long, interesting ones, I can't think. . . .

I wish you could have seen us Christmas eve. We sat up till twelve o'clock singing. Mr. Folsom sang many funny songs, among which was "Alonso the Brave," and "The Fair Imogene," which is part acted and part sung. After he had finished he was greeted with prolonged applause from the whole company, after which we drank a bumper of rhubarb wine and retired rather unsteadily to our several couches. . . .

We have been busy today constructing a fish-house, situated on the bank by Babb's Cove, close by the northeast corner of the swamp. We attempted to move the old one, which you remember was parted off into a fish room and bathing room, but while we were hauling it over a hill it fell down smash, so we were compelled to stave it to pieces.

About ten o'clock today Johnson came out bringing the mail, also a package for Mr. Folsom, and your last letter. Oh, you dear, why are you not more careful? It is no joke to break through the ice. You poor child, what an uncomfortable walk you must have had home. And then the other mishaps which befell you. It is altogether too bad. As for us, our lives glide on as smoothly as can be. There are no ponds deep enough to drown in if we do break through the ice—the water is not over our boots. The only accident which has happened to me lately is this. When we were getting the old bowling alley up, I happened to be prying with a crowbar, and suddenly the bar slipped and I fell plump upon my nose, which produced rather unpleasant sensations at the time, but it was soon over. . . .

A large ship passed by, to the westward, today. All sail was set but the upper sails, and she made a fine appearance. The poor little minnows, once inhabitants of the aquarium, are all gone, and we discovered the rascally sculpin devouring the last one, which was a most lamentable sight, I assure you. . . . Dear Sister, you must excuse this abominable letter; it is written in a hurry. Mr. Folsom encloses a letter for John. Good bye, you dear, and a very merry Christmas—written before I knew it—I meant to say Happy New Year. Once more good bye, and believe me

Affectionately,
Cedy

P.S. . . . Did you know Ben[1] is dead?

1. Ben: Thomas Laighton's assistant at the lighthouse, Ben Whaling, had afterwards continued as a man-of-all-work at Appledore. According to Oscar

in *Ninety Years,* Ben left "on a terrible tear" when Nancy Newton, who was Eliza Laighton's chief helper, married and moved to Star Island.

* * *January 2, 1861. Evening* * *

I commence a journal letter, for your especial benefit, though the idea of my writing anything which will interest you is ridiculous. This has been a most delightful day. The morning was a little cloudy, but it soon cleared off finely, and the sun shone bright and warm. . . . This afternoon we sailed over to Star Island and purchased four cusque fish. We had a nice little breeze and our boat glided over the water "like a thing of life." Mr. Folsom has deserted the parlor tonight for his room, where he has a wood stove. Mr. Manley is writing, so you see it is pretty quiet here just now. We have been annoyed lately by an old sheep that comes into the cellar directly under us, and coughs in the most horrible manner—the most unearthly sound I ever heard—quite frightful, I assure you. I have been thinking of your dream tonight. You just come here in reality. You would find the only danger to be that you'd be hugged and kissed to pieces. I observe a long heavy cloud over the western horizon, which Father used to call a "skim-cloud," and which is a pretty sure sign of unpleasant weather.

January 3rd, Evening. What an awful day this has been, has it not? Snow, snow, snow, all day long. This forenoon I went with Mr. Manley up to the billiard room and played several games of billiards. Two of the turkeys roosted out last night, and this morning their respectable countenances looked even bluer than usual. I never saw such silly birds. I saw two little humilities[1] down in the upper dock today. They seemed to be enjoying themselves immensely, wading in the cold water. Snowbanks begin to gather all around the house. . . . Father is reading "Great Expectations" this evening to Mother out in the kitchen. I suppose you know we take *Harper's Weekly,* principally because of the story. Mr. Folsom, Mr. Manley, Bocky and myself are in. Bocky and Mr. Manley are boxing, and though they are not very scientific, they manage to strike some pretty hard blows. They have just finished. Bocky cast Mr. Manley on the sofa, where he lies to recover his breath. Bocky has just taken his fiddle and is playing, or rather sawing, at a great rate.

January 4th. Three o'clock P.M. Johnson has just arrived with the mail and is about to return to Portsmouth. I finish this in haste that I may send it.

Ever affectionately,
Cedy

1. humilities: "Humility" was a popular name for the willet.

*   *   *January 5, 1861*   *   *

. . . January 7th. Rain—rather unusual for this time of year. It freezes as fast as it falls and the snow is crusted over as smooth as glass. I played several games of billiards today, and succeeded in winning them all. The wind has been northeast today, thermometer twenty-six. This morning I noticed one of our neighbors from Gosport on the big hill, trudging about through the snow in quest of wild fowl. Two of them who were over here the other day asked Bocky with much earnestness where we had moved the bowling alley, for they could not distinguish it among our numerous buildings. The addition of the shop makes quite a village.

Several grey gulls flew over the upper dock today. There are plenty of small gulls about now. They are very tame, with white wings tipped with black; they are called by the Islanders *meouls*,[1] are considered good to eat, and many of them are shot. Would you like some of their wings?

January 8th. Ten o'clock A.M. We are just going over to Star Island to carry the mail over, so I thought I would finish and send this.

Affectionately,
Cedy

1. *meouls*: This word, which Cedric later spells *meowls*, presents an identification problem. W. L. McAtee gives *meou* as a name for both the common and the Arctic tern ("Folk Names of New England Birds," *Mass. Audubon Society Bulletin*, Jan. 1956). But the tern does not winter in New

England, and it is doubtful that it did so in the 1860's. Furthermore, the tern was no stranger to the Laightons. Celia, in *Among the Isles of Shoals*, says, "I remember . . . when on Duck Island the 'medrakes,' or tern, made rude nests on the beach." Cedric, in his letter of June 14, 1863 (p. 53) writes, "The medrake or swallow-tailed gull is the only variety [of gull] that breeds at the island." Obviously the "meoul" was a newcomer.

It is my guess that he was observing the first incursions of the herring gull. Compared to the black-backed and the glaucous ("burgomaster") gulls, which were familiar winter visitors, the herring gull might well have seemed small to Cedric.

* * *January 9, 1861* * *

. . . January 12th. When we got up this morning, we found to our horror that it was snowing again—coming down in clouds and burying deeper and deeper the shrubs and bushes, which constitute our forests. The poor cows looked quite melancholy when we let them out, and eyed the falling snow with eyes that fairly spoke their despair. Bocky and I worked in the shop this forenoon. He is making a bird-cage and I moulded a lot of bullets for our pistols. Did you know we possessed pistols? Father presented us with one apiece last fall. They are revolving, and will shoot five times without being reloaded. . . .

Mother sends loads of love to all.

Ever affectionately,
Cedy

* * *January 18, 1861* * *

Dear Sister,

After a lapse of several days (several weeks it seems to me) the mail has arrived. . . . Mother is delighted with the little picture, and thinks there can be nothing more perfect. When I showed it to her, she exclaimed, "Isn't that precisely like her?" Bocky and I think it might be better, though it is the best likeness of you I have seen. What a darling little boy Lony[1] must be; it fairly caused the tears to come into my eyes when I read your account of his sweet, cunning little actions. How I should like to see him, and kiss him for a half hour at least. . . .

I wish you could hear Polly talk. She has really got to be a wonder, and says with great emphasis, "What you got in your pocket?" and "How are you?" The canaries are getting along finely. Bocky has made two cages for them, and they are perfectly happy.

Father said as I passed by where he was sitting, "Here, Cedy, take these papers into the parlor, the country has gone to the d——l!" It seems that the South is determined on disunion.

Three or four days ago a sloop-of-war passed by the Island from Portsmouth, bound south I guess, as the papers state that one passed Cape Cod lately. . . .

With loads of love to all, I remain ever

Affectionately,
Cedy

1. Lony: This was a family nickname for Roland, Celia's third and youngest child, who was born August 28, 1858.

* * *January 20, 1861* * *

Dear Sister,

Yesterday we made two trips to Star Island—the first one after Johnson and the second after fish. We started away as soon as we had finished dinner, and as we went round the point we saw a large ship being towed by a steam tug. It proved to be a salt ship bound to Portsmouth. We landed at Star Island, and having given the mail to Johnson's little boy, we rowed over to Smuttynose and jumped out into a snowbank (for you can't go anywhere without getting buried in snow these times), and proceeded to the fish-house, where we beheld a most heart-rending spectacle. It happened that the set-lines were in the fish-house, and had just been baited. A large white and black cat, attracted by the smell of fresh bait, went up to the line and began to eat; the consequence was she got hooked, and as we passed in she uttered the most piteous yells imaginable. John Poole was close by, so I called him and we proceeded to extricate the poor thing. After trying to get the hook out for a few minutes, Poole drew forth a long knife and began to cut it out, ejaculating as he did so, "Poor kitty, this ain't the first hook I've cut out of you, you poor thing." As soon as the hook was taken out, the cat vanished, never to be seen again by mortal eyes. As soon as we got home, Mother told us we must go over again and get some fish (the fishing boats were not in when we went the first time), so we started off again in quest of the fish. They were all aboard Johnson's vessel, so we went aboard of the *Lone Star* and got six haddocks, a cod, a catfish, and two cusques. "The shades of night were coming down swift" before we got them all cleaned and up to the house.

January 21. Evening. We are having a furious northwester at the present time; not a vessel has been seen today. The whitecapped waves are dashing upon Little Island and the western part of the Island with great fury. Of course there has been no chance to Portsmouth[1] today. The clothes which were hung out to dry this morning were taken from the lines with great expedition by the wind, and hurled far away down to Broad Cove—tablecloths, sheets, pantaloons, &c. went flying round in the wildest confusion. I found one tablecloth making rapid progress towards Norwegian Cove.

Mother brought Polly into the parlor this morning for the amusement of our friends, but the objects and surroundings were so entirely new that we could not prevail upon her to say a thing. The only thing she said was "Poor Poll" in the most dismal way imaginable.

January 22nd. Evening. This day has been pleasanter than I anticipated; we have had the sun all day and it has been moderately warm. We have been bottling cider today—filled about a hundred and fifty bottles. The cider is very nice, the best we ever had. Mr. Folsom and Mr. M. paid us a visit in the early part of the forenoon and assisted us. The shadows flitted fantastically around us in the dark old cellar. Sometimes the bottles which surrounded us on every side appeared to be having a dance "on their own hook," and seemed to stretch their long necks forward in anticipation of the sparkling draughts which awaited them. I filled the bottles, Mr. M. corked them, Bocky tied the corks down, and Mr. F. passed the bottles along to be filled. Mr. M., in the endeavor to cork one, drove the cork in so hard that the bottom gave in and the cider was spilled upon his best pantaloons. Wasn't that too bad? He did not mind it much though. Polly has been here about all day. Mother took her away a little while ago.

Johnson has not been seen today, and Mr. M. is getting impatient, for he wishes to be in Boston by Wednesday. We have just finished our supper, which consisted of delicious buttered toast and crabapples. . . .

January 25. Evening. . . . This afternoon, while we were here in the parlor, the *China* passed by in front, which reminded us that Johnson must be on the way; and as we expected a cow out by him, we ran up to Thirty-two and found he was close by, with the cow on the deck of his schooner. We rushed for the kitchen, and after putting on boots, coats, &c., we hauled down our boat and rowed out to meet him, first landing Mr. F. on Little Island, where he could see the operation of landing the cow. Johnson luffed his boat up by Little Island, on the north side, about twice as far as was needful, tied a rope around the cow's horns, and passing the end to his men, who were in his small boat, he, without waiting for us to come up, threw the cow overboard. The moment she struck the water Johnson commenced to swear in the most horrible manner. His crew consisted of two Swedes, and he is a Norwegian, you know. Such a jargon I never heard. "Pull, pull, pull!" screamed Johnson at the top of his voice, with an oath long, loud, and deep. (He was afraid the cow would drown.) The poor fellows were pulling as fast as they could, but I was not satisfied, so I asked Bocky to put me aboard of their boat. I jumped, and in my jump knocked the poor Swede off the seat (as I had intended), and grasping the oars, attempted to row. There were but two tholepins, one on a side. Bocky threw me some more out of his boat, I gave three strokes, and lo! the miserable oar broke, and I threw it to the four winds. Bocky gave me another oar and we went on again. All this time Johnson was swearing at a great rate; he didn't stop from the time the cow was thrown overboard till we reached the shore, which we did in safety. Even then we could hear him in the distance, yelling as if possessed of a fiend. After it was all over I laughed loud and long to think of the whole proceeding, which was comical in the extreme. The mail came, of course, and was brought in by one of the men after we had got the cow ashore.

Two long letters from you, you dear! for which accept my part of the thanks which are due you. And now I bring this wretched letter to a close.

Ever affectionately,
Cedy

1. chance to Portsmouth: Apparently a Shoals expression. Cedric uses it on other occasions.

* * *January 26, 1861* * *

Dear Sister,

This morning we went over to Star and Smuttynose Islands. This northeast wind carried our little boat along with great swiftness, and Mr. F. was delighted; he introduced wild projects, such as building a house on Duck Island, or Londoner,[1] and living at the islands all his life. At Smuttynose we selected from a pile of lumber on the wharf two planks with which to make door frames (for there is to be made an entry through the dining room, so people will not have to go out on the piazza to get from parlour to parlour). We then proceeded to Star Island in order to leave the mail for Johnson to take to Portsmouth.

Old Joe Caswell[2] met us on the shore. Do you know whom I mean?—the same man that showed Mrs. J. Dana Betty Moody's Cave[3] so long ago, and frightened her by carrying her little daughter in his arms. Bocky and I were with her, and I think you were with us too, am I right? At any rate we met him this morning, and I am sorry to say he was, to use a common expression, a little tight. After bidding us good morning, he said to Mr. F., "What do you do over there? I've got a spy-glass and I see you over on the snow most every day." Mr. F., not quite understanding, replied, "Oh, I am a Southerner." "A Southerner are ye?" said Old Joe. "I don't see what you want in this cold climate." Just then Bocky came down from Johnson's house and exclaimed, "Well, Uncle Joe, where is the Constitution and Union of the United States?" "Where is the Union?" ejaculated Old Joe, patting himself on the breast. "Here, in my heart!" "Supposing Gen Jackson was in the Chair," continued he, "do you think our vessels would be fired at, hey?" We shoved our boat off from the shore, and Old Joe shouted, "Tell your father to pitch into that man!" meaning Mr. F. After we got off far enough, we all burst into an explosion of laughter. Mrs. Johnson asked anxiously about the cow. She said her husband was very much worried; he thought the cow might have died from the effects of her cold bath.

We have been trying the old aeolian harp, which we used to have at White Island. It played beautifully, and Mr. F. fell asleep on the sofa listening to it. Our supper was brought in a few moments ago—the most delicious toast, made of raised bread. We fell to talking over it of last summer's adventures. Do you remember a man named Bigelow? who was always in the way, and people thought he would never go home? And then poor little Mrs. Flagg, and how her spouse went off in a leaky boat, which frightened her terribly? How folks did complain about those attic rooms. I never heard anything like it, and it is all to be gone through with again this summer, I suppose. . . .

January 27. Evening. . . . We have just been taking a peep at the moon through the spy-glass. How beautiful the moon is! White Island light must look splendidly from the hill this evening. Was the tower finished while you were here? I think it is much prettier than the old one, much more symmetrical. . . .

January 28. Evening. This day has been quite pleasant; if it was not for this confounded snow, we should enjoy ourselves pretty well. Bocky and I worked in the shop this forenoon, sawing plank into suitable lengths for door frames. Johnson has not been seen today. When we got up from our dinner, in the kitchen, we found one of the sheep in the dining room. The parlor doors happened to be open, which gave free admittance.

Mr. F. came in a few moments ago, very much excited. He had

been over to Blue Beach, and had caught four more of the little suckerfishes, and had also seen a large rat which he tried to kill but without success. We are arranging a series of expeditions after beasts, as Mr. F. designates the inhabitants of the aquarium. Sometime about the first of February the tides will be very low and will occur about the right time of day. Then we shall search every nook and corner after beasts. Mr. F. is desirous to get a butterfish; there used to be lots of them in Babb's Cove, but there are none to be found now. The aquarium is getting along nicely. I forgot to mention the addition of a sculpin, a little larger than the other one.

Mr. F. and Bocky just had a bout with the gloves; Mr. F. sank upon the sofa several times, not because he wished to, but because Bocky's furious blows compelled him to seek that locality for safety. Mother has been trying the sewing machine lately; sometimes it works pretty well, and at others there is no doing anything with it. About forty needles have been broken, and all the patience that was ever possessed, exhausted. You know what it is, as you have tried it. We sent to Boston by Mr. Manley for a new lot of needles, but whether he will get them there or not remains to be seen. . . .

January 29. Evening. Thank the Lord, this month is most past. We examined the weather record today and found that in fourteen days out of twenty-nine there have been snowstorms. . . . May the Lord send rain, boiling hot! . . . I am sorry I cannot get any terrible accident that would interest you. It would be a nice thing if we could have a collision of vessels or something of the sort, but there is nothing new in our world (which is Appledore), so I will bid you good night. . . .

Ever affectionately,
Cedy

1. Duck Island, or Londoner: As far as we know, both islands were uninhabited at that time. A deserted shanty stood on Duck, substantial enough to house a ghost (See Celia Thaxter, *Among the Isles of Shoals*). Probably Londoner had no house, though Thomas Leehee was to build one a few years later.

There are many variants of the name *Londoner*. Tradition has it that a fishing company from London was based there in early colonial days; hence *Londoners*, the most usual form in Cedric's period. Now it is commonly

Lunging, and I have even seen it written *Luncheon*. These latter names appear to have evolved from *London* in the same way that *Indian* has turned into *Injun*.

2. Old Joe Caswell: Joseph M. Caswell, born July 21, 1800. He was Star Island's first innkeeper of record, having been host to Richard Henry Dana, Jr. when he visited the islands in 1843. The occasion when Caswell took a Mrs. J. Dana to Betty Moody's Cave was probably somewhat later.

3. Betty Moody's Cave: A natural hiding place in the trapdike on the east side of Star Island. The legend is that Mrs. Moody, wife of the Gosport minister, hid herself and her children there during an Indian raid in 1724. In stifling her baby's cries, Betty smothered the baby but saved the rest of the family.

* * *February 3, 1861* * *

Dear Sister,

. . . Yesterday afternoon was very foggy; at times Little Island was scarcely discernable. There was a light breeze to the northwest, and just after dinner we started off in our boat to carry the mail over to Star Island. We sailed, as we usually do when there is wind enough. Mr. Folsom steered the boat, an occupation of which he is very fond—he considers it excellent fun. We arrived at the Island all safe, and on starting to come home we observed that the fog was very thick and was driving in between the islands in great clouds. We had scarcely pulled a dozen strokes when the land became invisible.

Mr. F. was mystified. We kept telling him how to steer, and at last he exclaimed, "Let me alone, and I'll steer right." "All right," said we, and on we went. After the lapse of several minutes we descried land ahead and a triumphant smile on the visage of Mr. F. We quickly approached the land, and it was Smuttynose.

You may be sure we laughed a little, and Bocky related the following anecdote. He said that several years ago he happened to be rowing a boatload of people from Smuttynose to this island. It was a little foggy at the time; no land could be seen; and the passengers began to look alarmed and anxiously asked Bocky if he thought he could find the way. "Have you a compass?" said Bocky, with an air of great wisdom. One of the passengers instantly responded by producing a small pocket compass, which was laid upon one of the thwarts. Bocky rowed on, frequently casting his eyes on that wonderful instrument, the compass, which was to decide the fate of the party. Suddenly the fog lifted a little, and lo! they were quietly rowing out to sea, having passed between this island and Smuttynose. The idea of losing one's way in the roads is rather ridiculous. . . .

The time is fast approaching when we shall have to put the cows in the barn, so I will bid you good bye, you dear.

Ever affectionately,
Cedy

* * *February 15, 1861* * *

Dear Sister,

. . . Yesterday was lovely. The ocean was as smooth as glass, not a ripple to be seen on the whole expanse of water. Numerous shoals of pollock were playing and jumping about in the direction of Londoner, and just above them swarmed thousands of meouls and gulls. The mainland was partially shrouded in mist, or rather haze, such as we often see in summer. The air was very mild, and Mother was so enchanted with the prospect that she determined to take a row. Bocky and I launched the boat, and presently Mother and Eliza came down to the wharf and we started. We proceeded to Star Island first, and there we secured the blessed mail of Mrs. Jansen, and then rowed over to Smuttynose.

The very minute we arrived, the Smuttynoseans of the female kind began to flock down to the boat to see Mother. They came from all quarters, and for a little while Mother was overwhelmed with questions. I retired to a neighboring fish-house, and was soon joined by Joseph Caswell, Jr., who made a few original remarks in regard to the gathering. "There they school," said he, as several more women joined the crowd. "I never saw the women congregate so," he continued, "without having a terrible storm immediately after." Just then, as if to verify his prediction, a chilly southeast wind sprang up, and the black clouds began to gather in every direction. Those heavy black clouds which portend hurricanes were piled up in the whole eastern sky, ready to burst upon this already snow deluged earth. After Mother had conversed with the aristocracy of Smuttynose for a short time, we started for home, where we arrived all safe, and all much pleased with the excursion. It is the first time Mother has been out this winter, and she enjoyed the fresh air and beautiful ocean scenery very much.

Verily Joe's prophecy is fulfilled, for the storm is coming down upon us with giant strength. The wind blows with the fury of a tornado, and the waves are dashing upon the eastern shores with great fury. If this wind continues twenty-four hours longer, the sea will probably break over the bank at Broad Cove. Oh that Mr. Folsom was here; again he is missing a sight of which we can seldom boast. I wish you were here too, you dear, for I know you would like to see the enormous billows rush in upon the old iron rocks, as you saw them long ago when you were with us. Do you remember the great April storm?[1] Of course you do. Didn't the waves look grand then? And didn't we enjoy it? . . .

Ever affectionately,
Cedy

Feb. 16th. I write this little addition to inform you of the arrival of our friends, Messrs. F. and M. They came this forenoon with Jansen.

1. See note, p. 40.

* * *February 26, 1861* * *

Dear Sister,

    We have had such a delightful and successful hunt for beasts that I thought I would give you an account of it. We started for the long point of Babb's Cove about half an hour before sunset. The tide was very low, and all the little pools which are usually hidden were open to search. We stopped at the Landing, and began to examine the ledge which juts out into Babb's Cove. The first thing we found was a sea-spider—a very large one. Then came some small crabs, and then two or three whelks. Just then I happened to move the seaweed, and I observed a shell on the bottom of the pond make a quick movement. I put my hand down and grasped it, and lo! it was a hermit crab. Mr. F. was delighted and fairly screamed for joy when I held the hermit crab up for inspection. I was so elated with my success that I determined to confine my efforts to the finding of hermit crabs, for they are certainly the most wonderful little creatures that inhabit our shores. I looked carefully on the bottom of every pond, and in a few minutes I found three more of the little fellows, one of which had grown nearly too large for his shell, and half of his body was hanging out. While I was catching the hermit crabs, Mr. Folsom had discovered and secured two moss crabs, a butterfish, lots of little limpets and urchins, and the "Lord knows what."

    By this time it began to grow dark, for the sun was down; and though there was a magnificent glow at the west, which extended from Portsmouth lighthouses away round to Newburyport, the shades of night began rapidly to descend, and we started for home. What with the excitement of beast-hunting and the glory of the evening, Mr. F. was in an enviable state of bliss. This has been the most beautiful day on record. A gentle southwest wind, which just stirs the water into a ripple, has been blowing here all day. The thermometer, even now at nine o'clock, stands at thirty-nine. About half an hour ago, Mr. Folsom and Mr. Manley went up on the southeast part of the big hill[1] to see the moon rise. They have just returned, and describe it as being a lovely spectacle. It rises so far to the southward that we can't see it from the parlor windows, as the hill hides it.

Bocky and Mr. M. are playing chess. Bocky exhibits his usual skill in that noble game and is beating his opponent with the greatest ease. Last night I played two games with Mr. Folsom; he won one game and I won the other, though not without a hard struggle. Do you ever play now? . . .

February 27. Evening. Did you ever experience such a pleasant day? Nearly all day the ocean has been perfectly calm. Soon after breakfast we started for a trip to White Island, where we arrived after a pleasant row. On the way over we saw many schools of pollock playing around Halfway Rock,[2] and now and then great numbers of them passed under the boat. White Island is changed somewhat, but many of the old places where we used to play when we were children were recognizable. The little platform which supports the capstan, at the south end of the boathouse, was particularly familiar. Do you remember how we used to play catch fish off that very platform?

After we had examined the lighthouse, we went over to the eastern part of the island, where the rocks are so precipitous. There we sat down on the rocks and gazed upon the placid ocean. The surf broke musically upon the rocks beneath us, as the tiny waves rushed in from the sea. Mr. Folsom was entranced with the beauty of the scene, and could hardly tear himself away. While we were out there we were joined by a large black cat, which came from the house and seemed to enjoy herself as much as any of us. On the way home we stopped at Londoner and there we filled our pockets with shells of every description. When we got home it was past two o'clock, and Father was out on the piazza keeping guard, and Mother had an excellent dinner prepared for us—to which we did justice, for the row had sharpened our appetites to an unlimited degree.

February 28. . . . Early this morning Mr. F. rowed over to Star Island alone, and sailed back. He enjoyed himself much, and brought mail and everything we sent for. . . . Just after breakfast, while Bocky and I were at work out by the barn, Mr. Folsom came rushing out with Mr. Manley's *Atlantic* magazine for March, and pointed triumphantly at a poem.[3] I recognized it in an instant, as I have a duplicate in my desk. It seems better than ever in print, and the title is very appropriate. Mother is delighted. Mr. F. read the one I have to her a short time ago, and she cried like a child. I don't know why she did, I'm sure; everything is for the best.

Just before dinner a small boat ran up into the upper dock, and Thomas Lee[4] (one of the Smuttynoseans) stepped upon the shore with another bundle of mail, and in it was a jolly letter from you. Poor Mr. Folsom was again disappointed, for there was nothing for him. Mr. Manley got four more letters. He thinks the parody[5] is very good; Father, however, doesn't think so much of it. . . .

There is an old coasting vessel beating up to Boston, off to the westward. Do you recollect when Mr. T. and Bocky were picked up by a coaster off Old York? I have always had great respect for coasting vessels ever since. . . .

Ever affectionately,
Cedy

1. See note, p. 44.
2. Halfway Rock: A hazard to local navigation, visible only at low tide, lying between Lunging and Star Islands.
3. poem: "Land-locked." See p. 6.
4. Thomas Lee: This name has several variant spellings in Cedric's letters and elsewhere, such as Leehee, Leigh, etc. Cedric often refers to Tom as Tom Tom or Tam Tam. A few years later, Lee built the house on Lunging (Londoners) Island now owned by the Randalls of Danvers, Mass.
5. On the back of Cedric's letter of February 15 is a parody of "Abou Ben Adhem" in Celia's handwriting. This was apparently the first draft of the verses which Celia copied and sent to Appledore. The first line is: "James Buchanan, may his tribe decrease. . . ."

* * *March 7, 1861* *

Dear Sister,

. . . Since I last wrote to you, the affairs of the aquarium have undergone an entire change. One morning when we took our accustomed look at it, we saw to our dismay that everything had died during the night except the hermit crabs, and that they were most gone. One of them was entirely out of his shell—he had come out to die according to their custom when death is approaching. We took them all out and put them into a pail of fresh salt water. . . . Mr. Folsom felt very much grieved about the aquarium, but he soon rallied, and took it down to the water with the intention of cleaning it out. He soon returned with a woebegone countenance, and facetiously remarked that he had finished the aquarium forever—broken it into a thousand pieces. We all laughed heartily, and Mr. F. laughed with us. . . .

Ever affectionately,
Cedy

* * *March 11, 1861* *

Dear Sister,

. . . Jansen came out today bringing the mail &c. No letters from you. Mr. Folsom sent to Boston for a new aquarium, and the letters which he has received lately inform him that it is in Portsmouth. Jansen said he called twice at the express office, but each time it was shut up; so we were disappointed of getting it today. There is but one hermit crab living now. The others indulged in several pitched battles, and losing nearly all their arms, they died the deaths of martyrs.

I suppose Bocky told you that Mr. Manley has departed.

Have you heard a tune called "Dixie Land"? It is sung a great deal now, I believe. It has a magical effect upon the listener. The hand-organ owners, so the papers say, are altering their instruments to the tune of Dixie, and are making their independent fortunes. . . .

Ever affectionately,
Cedy

* * *April 7, 1861* * *

Dear Sister,

. . . I am writing upstairs in our room. I can look from the east window upon yours and my friend, the ever pleasant sea. Whether in storm or calm, the sea is always pleasant to me. This morning the waves reverberate around Broad Cove with a joyful sound. After all, what better companion can one have than the ocean—it talks to you when you wish to talk, and is silent when you wish for silence. I don't wonder you love it. However, the hardy mariners who have to breast the fierce storms and gales which beset them would very likely give a different opinion in regard to it. Some sailors, though, love the sea, I am quite sure.

. . . A few nights ago I went to bed pretty early. I did not feel very sleepy, so I took a book containing "The Raven," by Edgar A. Poe, and before I went to sleep I had learned it all by heart. Do you remember the poem I refer to? Bocky says you used to repeat it to him a long while ago. I think it is a remarkable production. There is a certain something about it that enchains one to the end. It is only with feelings of melancholy that one can look back upon this gifted author's career, which was brought to so ignominious a termination. Mr. Folsom read us some of his prose works last winter, among which was "The Gold Bug," which is a story of thrilling interest. All his stories seem to have a tendency toward the marvellous.

You asked me in your last letter to continue the journal correspondence. I assure you it is impossible to do so, for we are *very* busy now, preparing for visitors. As Bocky very originally expresses himself, "We shall have to keep everything snapping to get through with our spring work." By the way, Higginson, in his "April Days" (in the last *Atlantic*) mentions a friend of his with the initials L. T. Does he mean Mr. Thaxter? Bocky received a magnificent circular saw from Charlestown[1] the other day, and he is immensely gratified. He is going to fix a balance wheel pretty soon, and then we shall see a circular saw in operation. Bocky has a liking for machinery of all kinds. For the past week we have been engaged in erecting a fence around the garden, to keep the sheep out. Yesterday we found several ledges in the very places where we wished to plant our posts, so we were forced to drill them, and put in a charge of powder. When we touched it off, great was the explosion!

Dear Sister, will you excuse this wretched letter? Mother and Father and Bocky send love. On the other side I am going to put a puzzle. You probably have seen it before.

Ever affectionately,
Cedy

1. Undoubtedly a gift from cousin Christopher Rymes. See note, p. 33.

* * May 3, 1861 * *

Dear Sister,

It is just nine o'clock here. Bocky is out in the shop busy with his circular saw, and as I have a little spare time at this moment, I begin a little letter for your special edification. Your kind letter dated April 25th has been duly received, for which please accept our thanks.

As you rightly guessed, we have been very busy this spring. However, we are most through now. One interminable job has been the sawing and the slitting of the old wood which lies scattered all over the island in every direction, and which accumulates at an astonishing rate in every nook and corner. We have sawed and split about four cords of it, and there is some of it left now.

The garden is nearly finished. We have planted any given quantity of potatoes, beets, &c. The cabbages are up—but whether this cold weather will kill them or not is a question. This morning we found ice three-quarters of an inch thick! I have got some flower seed which I intend to plant by the cottage. Dog-tooth violets and anemones are to be found in great profusion now. The little blue violets have not made their appearance yet, though the leaves have started.

What a terrible thing this war is, isn't it? I think it is quite impossible for the Southerners to hold out long against the enormous number of men and powerful equipment of the North.

God grant there will be as little bloodshed as possible. We are so isolated here that we hear comparatively little about the events which are daily occurring on the mainland. It is true that the papers tell us, but that is not like hearing people talk about these things, and seeing the demonstrations of patriotism. I wish you could hear our neighbor, Daniel Webster, talk politics. I see the blessed stars and stripes are floating triumphantly over the fish-house at Star Island.

Father, Bocky, and I have all been suffering with sore throats and all the attendant evils of bad colds for the past few days. We are getting better now.

I suppose you have seen Mr. Folsom before this time, though you had not when you wrote last. We had a great carousal the night before he went away. We demolished a whole bottle of catawba wine, and yet we didn't get drunk; though, to be sure, Bocky danced more than was necessary, and I felt rather sleepy.

There are two joiners here now. They are fixing the bowling alley up nicely. I believe we have got those wretchedly crooked alleys straight at last. . . .

With much love to all, I am your

Affec. brother,
Cedy

*   *   *May 19, 1861*   *   *

Dear Sister,

This is a lovely day. I have been over on the southeast part of the island after dandelions. I was very successful, procuring a large basketful. The island is beginning to put on a new dress—all the bushes are leaving out, and the fields are bright with grass. . . . Houstonias, too, begin to dot the ground. And this morning I gathered a large handful of those cunning little blue violets. I believe there is but one place on the island where they grow, and that is on the little hill.

I have received two letters from Mr. Folsom since he left the island. He writes from the camp and the battlefield, and is full of military matters. Your letter to me and one for Bocky have been received. Many thanks for the cockades, you dear Sister—they are very gay.

Father has been sick for a week past, but is now getting better.

The bowling alley is finished, and the bathing house is nearly completed. The bathing house is situated near the place where the bowling alley used to be, only a little farther up toward the cottage. It is built very low, so it does not intercept the view much. It will be an improvement to have a good bathing house, I think.

The things look finely in the garden—the potatoes are up, while in the bed beets, onion, parsley, carrots, lettuce, and sage have sprouted. The weeds, too, are preparing to make a vigorous onslaught upon our time and patience. Weeding is a very disagreeable job, I think.

We have launched one of our whale-boats, and Mother, Bocky, and I intend to take a trip to Portsmouth pretty soon, in order to purchase the necessary goods for the summer.

Hoping to hear from you soon, I am, most affectionately, your brother,

Cedy

* * *May 30, 1861* * *

Dear Sister,

Your pleasant letter of the 18th was received some time ago, and I should have answered it sooner, but we have been so busy, and I have felt so tired every night, that I could scarcely hold my head up. I wish you could see our garden just now; it looks finely. The potatoes are six inches high, and we have had several large bunches of lettuce for salad. The weeds, though, are terribly thick, and require constant attention. . . .

Father got a letter from R. A. Preble last March, in which he said he would run the *Sibyl* this year, the same as last year. Since then we have heard but little from him, and whether his boat will run or not I am unable to inform you. At any rate, the packet, whether the *Sibyl* or any other boat, will commence to run on the 20th of June. Dear Sister, how delighted we all should be to see you; I hope you will be able to come early.

Mother has been rather unwell lately, with neuralgia in her knee. This neuralgia is very troublesome to Mother—for a few days she was scarcely able to walk.

I got a letter from Mr. Folsom today. He has been promoted in the ranks of the drill club, and quaintly remarks that we shall soon have to address him as "Dear General."

Dear Sister, please excuse this rapidly written epistle, and believe me ever,

Affectionately,
Cedy

* * June 11, 1861 * *

Dear Sister,

Your kind letter from the dancing school was duly received, and tonight another one came dated the 9th. We are all delighted to hear you are coming. I do not think there is any doubt about it now. Mr. Preble was out here a short time ago, and Father made all the arrangements about running his boat—so you will have a splendid boat to come from Portsmouth in.

We have been having some very fine weather here. The Island is covered with little Houstonias, and the swamps are blue with flower-de-luce. Last Thursday—or Wednesday, I think it was—Bocky, Eliza, and I went to Portsmouth. The city of Portsmouth was in a high state of excitement; troops were continually marching through the streets, and down by Fort Constitution we saw quite a body of soldiers drilling. The guns on the forts are unhoused, and ready for use. The *Santee* and two other vessels of war are lying at the Navy Yard. These vessels are nearly ready for sea, I believe.

This forenoon we sheared the sheep, and such a bleating as they kept up was never before heard. There were forty-five of them, and we finished them before we ate our dinner.

We have got an old turkey with a brood of ducklings. Did you ever hear of such a thing? The turkey mother takes excellent care of them, and exhibits some signs of distress when they go into the water. We've got about twenty young turkeys, all flourishing.

There are any quantity of strawberries over on Duck Island. About the time you get here they will be ripe, and we will go down and get some. Now I guess you'll come!

The aquarium is still alive, and the hermit crabs are lively as ever. There are nine hermit crabs, a butterfish, a moss crab, and several other little creatures in it.

In none of my letters have I answered your question about Father's cockade. I do not think it is much use to make one; he'll never wear it.

Father, Mother, and Bocky join me in sending loads of love.

Affectionately,
Cedy

* * *July 6, 1861* * *

Dearest Sister,

... After you left in the wagon, I went up to Mr. Moses' store and paid the bill against Sedrek Laton. And then I went aboard the salt ship lying at Pier Wharf, and saw there some goats, the first I ever saw, for I do not remember those we used to have at White Island. ...

The *Sibyl* did not bring anybody yesterday—not one passenger, and four went away from here. Christie and Myra[1] are still here, but are going Monday.

We carried the last of the hay into the barn yesterday, and I celebrated the event by drinking a couple of bottles of spruce beer.

Please give my love to Mr. Folsom and Mr. Thaxter and the dear children, and believe me ever,

Aff.
Cedy

1. Christie and Myra: Cedric's cousin, Christopher Rymes, and his wife. Christie had lived on Appledore while the hotel was being built, his father, "Uncle William," having been in charge of the workmen. The family subsequently moved to Bow Street in Portsmouth. Christopher went on to become a distinguished civil engineer in Massachusetts, with a home in Somerville and an office in Charlestown. He was most considerate of the island cousins, particularly of their needs in mechanical equipment. Two years before, he had given Oscar a foot lathe.

Myra also was their cousin, nee Almira Laighton Cheever, the daughter of Joseph Cheever and Thomas Laighton's sister Deborah. It was Cheever who had taken Laighton's place for a time as lighthouse keeper.

* * *July 7, 1861* * *

Dear Sister,

Just after I had sent that short note of yesterday, Mother came to me and asked whether I had mentioned Abby Smith. I answered "No." And today, agreeable to her wish, I write to inform you that the said Abby Smith is a very kind, pleasant, and efficient person, and that Mother likes her very much. Mother thinks she will be a great help to her this summer.

Yesterday the *Sibyl* brought out several passengers, among whom was John G. Whittier. Also some of his friends. I carried them over to church today, and while I was waiting for them, I heard a man describing a certain singer he had heard. "Oh, she was a splendid singer," said he; "she could sing from away up to sixteen degrees above *sorrer* down to a double bass." . . .

Love to all.

          Ever aff.,
          Cedy

* * *July 16, 1861* * *

Dear Sister,

. . . Ben Gilbert has been staying here some time, and every day since he has been here he has gone out fishing. Yesterday he returned with a codfish weighing fifty-one pounds! Just think of it! It reminded one of a young whale. Ben did not catch it himself, though—it was caught by one of his party.

There have been lots of mackerel round lately, and the Gosportians have taken several hundred barrels of them. We have had them every day for a week, and very nice they are, being fat and juicy.

I carried a party over to Rye the other day, and went up to the Ocean House—the first time I ever was there. The house is fitted up in grand style, and the walks among the trees are very pretty, but the bowling alley and billiard table very defective, particularly the billiard table. . . .

Mother is continually sounding the praises of Abby Smith. And indeed, one can see that she is a great help by the difference in Mother, who now feels relieved of some of the responsibility and care which has for so many years devolved upon her. . . .

There are about twenty people here now. Franklin Pierce[1] came down a short time ago, and went back the same day. . . .

Affectionately,
Cedy

1. Franklin Pierce: At this time an ex-President, Pierce had been one of Thomas Laighton's first guests, having registered at the Mid Ocean House on Smuttynose in 1846, just before serving in the Mexican War. He was responsible for bringing his old college classmate, Hawthorne, to the Shoals.

* * *September 30, 1861* * *

Dear Sister,

Your kind letter of the 22nd was received some time ago, and I should have answered it before, but something or other has happened every day to prevent until now. The day that it arrived, we were unusually busy—a schooner-load of wood (twenty cords) was being landed at the wharf, and Bocky & Tom & I had to take it up by the piazza as fast as it was thrown ashore. . . .

We are all gratified to hear of the success of your poem. Please send both of them in your next letter; I am eager to read them.

The work of building[1] is still going on, though rather slowly. The foundation is nearly laid, and the rock framework of a tank sixteen feet long & fifteen feet wide by six feet deep is made so the house will be built over it. In excavating for the tank and foundation, an immense pile of earth and rocks had to be removed, which was no light job. Every now and then while we were digging, the men who were blasting the ledge would shout, "Out of the pit," and away we would scamper up to the eastern end of the cottage for safety. In a moment the charge would explode, and earth, timber, and rocks would go flying in the air hundreds of feet. The blasting has been going on for over a fortnight, and though the ledge is pretty well shattered, it is not all removed yet, and some parts are as firm as ever. We expect the lumber for the building every day. It is to be sent direct from Bangor, Maine, in schooners. Five of the joiners are here, ready to receive it when it does come.

I believe Bocky wrote you some account of the magnificent proceedings here at Appledore on my birthday. All the people stopping at the house were exceedingly kind to me. Miss Adie Bigelow made me a present of a very pretty little picture, illustrating Whittier's poem, "Maud Muller." The picture is Maud Muller herself. Miss B.'s little brother Joseph also sent me a present of a small portemonnaie. Mr. E. W. Rollins and his excellent mother gave me presents, and Mr. J. Morse and lady gave me several books. Altogether I was treated with great kindness. None were kinder than my dear mother, though, who made some exquisite cake, the wherewithal to celebrate my twenty-first birthday.

Miss Westcott is still with us, though she intends to return to her home within a few days. Indications of the coming winter begin to be seen. The cold nights we have been having lately have changed the leaves on the hills to purple and yellow, and though it is very pretty to look at, it sets one to thinking sadly of the dreary snowstorms that are coming. This morning I saw the first loon gliding over the water in front of the house. The gulls, also, begin to fly from and to Duck Island. If I get a chance at one of them this winter, rest assured I shall not forget you.

And now, dearest Sister, good night! I am up in our room seated at a big table, which Bocky's forethought has lately added to our furniture. Bocky sits opposite me, scribbling to some friend with might and main.

Imagine that you hear the voices of Father, Mother, and brothers, united, when I again say good night and God bless you.

Affectionately,
Cedy

1. The work of building: This construction, which continued through the winter, was the first major expansion of the hotel. The new unit, between the main house and the North Cottage, would include forty rooms and a dance hall.

*   *   *October 22, 1861*   *   *

Dear Sister,

It seems an age since your kind letter was received; I don't know really how long it is, but I know I ought to have answered it before this. Every day from sunrise to sunset there is something to occupy our hands and minds. The ledge, I am glad to inform you, is demolished! It was a grand undertaking, and has improved the appearance of things immensely. The fragments of the ledge were deposited in the low ground between the barn and the main buildings. A heavy covering of earth (obtained in digging the trenches) brings the whole level with the surrounding ground. Bocky, who has worked on it today, says that about three hours more will finish the framing. I have been piling wood all day. Two men with wheelbarrows bring it into the woodshed, and I pile it snugly away, so that the small wood-house may hold the twenty cords. Pip[1] has assisted me in my arduous task, and amused me very much by his quaint sayings. He said, "I wish Mr. Folsom would come down with another box of oranges." I told him that I should be very glad to see Mr. Folsom whether he brought any oranges or not. "Why," said he, "don't you love oranges?"

Mother has gone to Portsmouth! That little sentence comprises all the misery and woe of Appledore. She went last Tuesday, and I suppose the very boat that takes this letter in will bring dear Mother from that wretched Portsmouth. Father has been wretched, and Bocky has been wretched, and I have been wretched ever since she has been gone.

Bocky and I have received several letters from Mr. Folsom lately. In his last he asks, "How is my gorgeous old friend, Poll?" Which reminds me of his patient care in teaching the bird new words last winter. What jolly times we used to have, . . . and how kind, good, and patient Mr. Folsom was throughout.

The new poem is splendid, but in my poor opinion *Landlocked* is better. I discover new beauties in *Land-locked* every day. I read it night before last, and was particularly charmed with the last two verses. Bocky says in his comic way that people used to come to him last summer and say, "Your sister writes for the magazines, doesn't she?" Many thanks for sending it. . . .

As it is growing rather late, I will close this letter by wishing you good night and pleasant dreams.

Ever affectionately,
Cedy

1. Edwin Foote Caswell, youthful member of a Rye family. He had recently joined the Laighton household to replace Ben Whaling.

* * *November 9, 1861* * *

Dear Sister,

Your long & pleasant letter of the first was received today. We were all glad to hear from you, as it is some time since you last wrote. Bocky & I have been lathing today. I have been lathing the ceiling, & my neck feels as though it had been twisted in all imaginable ways—however, we shall have a chance to rest tomorrow. The first story of the house is twelve feet high, which will give a nice high ceiling for the big parlor. The joiners have been to work all the week on the window frames, which they have just completed. The next thing to do will be clapboarding, and then the outside will begin to look pretty. Father has got the paint for the outside, & he intends to paint it a *beau-ti-ful* lemon color. Among our assistants is a regular painter by the name of Fred Akerman, who will help us paint when the time comes, & show us how to do it properly. Dear Mother has been cleaning the old kitchen today. Fred whitewashed the walls, & it looks as bright & pleasant as can be. I have got to love that old kitchen. The time that I have spent in it has endeared every object it contains. There is something lasting & permanent about it. I trust it will never be changed.

The storm of Saturday & Sunday, a week ago, raged fearfully here. It was second only to the great April storm of eighteen hundred and fifty-three.[1] Saturday afternoon the ocean was comparatively still, but Sunday the sea had risen so much that it came through & over Broad Cove with great fury. We hauled up many of our small boats lying on the shore after the waves had reached them. We thought they were perfectly safe, but the waves rolled nearly up to the cherry tree. I wish you could have taken a peep at it. Duck Island was entirely submerged, & Mingo Rock[2] threw the spray off beautifully. The waves rushed around Smutty so fiercely that the whole of the woodwork of the wharf was carried away. Shingles were torn off of the fish-houses at Star, which had remained untouched by the sea for years. We had two boats out on the moorings, but they rode out the gale safely. It seems that this very storm wrecked a large ship somewhere off Boston. You have probably seen some account of it. All of the crew but seven were lost.

The picture of the autumn leaves is a perfect wonder. Manley and a couple of friends who are paying the Shoals a short visit examined them (the picture) the other day, & thought it very perfect. Mr. Manley was quite sure, at first, that real leaves were stuck on the paper. Bocky made the same mistake. Mother is greatly delighted, & requests that you will thank Miss Robbins[3] in the most cordial manner for her. . . .

November 10. This day has been very pleasant. Sundays, somehow or other, are always pleasant. Nothing of importance has happened today except the arrival of a package of mail matter. Did I tell you that old Lem had attempted to commit suicide again? and in the same way? I guess he has succeeded this time. We heard yesterday that he was failing very fast.

A very singular thing happened while Mother was in Portsmouth. You know that Mother almost always stays at Aunt Maria's[4] house. Well, one afternoon there happened to be a lady visiting there who was a medium (spiritual medium), and while they were all sitting quietly in the front room, this lady was influenced by the spirit of old Ben.[5] The lady held a slate in her hands, and the first manifestation was the drawing of a pair of lamp scissors precisely like the ones Ben used to use. The next thing was the old knife-cleaner, which was made very perfectly. Mother said, "What does that mean?" and instantly Benjamin was written. Then a garden fork was made, and then beds with little vegetables growing in them. If this was the spirit of old Ben, he could not have chosen a better way to make himself known.

November 11. We have been lathing steadily all day. This morning was quite pleasant, but about ten o'clock the clouds gathered in the southwest, and pretty soon down came the rain in torrents. This afternoon a large white owl lit on the black ledge by the upper dock, but I forbore to shoot him, as he will probably kill a great many rats before he leaves the island. I shot two gray gulls the other day, but the white ones, being older and more experienced, do not trust themselves within range of a gun that never misses. However, I shall get a chance at them before the winter goes by.

I shall probably get a chance to send this letter in tomorrow, so I guess I will end it here.

Father, Mother, & Bocky join me in sending loads of love.

Ever aff.,
Cedy

1. the great April storm of 1853: The storm was actually in 1851, although Celia remembered it as 1849 in *Among the Isles of Shoals*. Oscar gave his own recollection of the event and got the date right too. In *Ninety Years at the Isles of Shoals,* he wrote:

> In April of the year 1851, the fiercest northeast storm in a hundred years swept the New England coast. The sea went clear

across both valleys of Appledore, making it look like three islands. Father was worried fearing the hotel would be swept away. Our boats under the piazza were afloat. Seaweed and rocks were washed up to the doors. This was the awful storm when, on the 17th of April, Minot's Ledge Light went down and the keepers were drowned. Our Valley of Fairyland ends on the east in Neptune's Hall, and on the west in Sandpiper Cove. The sea had gone through this valley, carrying away our little house. The blackbird must have been astonished when he returned that spring to find his nesting place covered with seaweed. The Star Islanders lost three boats in this gale, and the Becker boys at Smuttynose had a struggle to save their fishing schooner in Smuttynose Dock, the safest harbor at the Islands.

2. Mingo Rock: A rock southeast of Duck Island.

3. Miss Robbins: Ellen Robbins (1828-1905) was a painter who also taught art in Boston and Watertown. She was best known for her paintings of flowers and still-life.

4. Aunt Maria: Eliza Laighton's sister, Lucy Maria (Rymes) Hoyt, the wife of Winthrop Hoyt. Mrs. Hoyt was born January 26, 1798.

5. old Ben: The late Ben Whaling. See note, p. 11.

* * *December 4, 1861* * *

Dear Sister,

. . . We have had a variety of occupations today. First we repaired a pump, & then we fixed a tank, & then we went up into the upper story of the new house & lathed till dinner. After dinner we helped carry into the building some eight or ten thousand feet of floor-boards, & then we went over to Star Island, carrying Almira (one of our assistants), that she might get a chance to Portsmouth. When we got back the sun was setting, & it was time to milk the cows. Bocky is out in the shop tonight working on his electrical machine, which, I think, will be a very handsome one. Bocky got while he was in Portsmouth a very pretty little parlor stove, which we have set up in this room. We have got all our pictures up here, & it looks quite gay. Perhaps you remember that we three first slept in this room when we moved from White Island. It seems a long time ago.

Amos Jenness[1] (one of the joiners) professes to predict the weather with undeviating accuracy. The other evening, while we were out of doors, he turned his eyes heavenward & said, "Tomorrow the wind will be west." "How do you know?" asked we. "Because," he responded, "that thing" (pointing upwards) "points east & west." He meant the Milky Way! At the time the wind was S.E. & it was raining, but in the morning it was clear, & the wind was directly west, as he had predicted. It seems a queer idea to take the Milky Way (millions of miles off) for a weather-cock. . . .

Ever affectionately,
Cedy

1. Amos Jenness: A carpenter from Rye, frequently employed by the Laightons. In *Ninety Years*, Oscar says of him:
> He was the most pessimistic old fellow I ever met, or perhaps "cranky" would be a better term. I had a kit of tools and helped him with the work that winter. One day Amos and I had a little difference as to how a door should be hung, and Amos exclaimed: "What do you know, you never saw an apple tree in blowth!" That was true enough, and he might have added that "You never saw a locomotive."

* * *December 12, 1861* * *

Dear Sister,

. . . We have been having some magnificent weather here. Last Monday was a very beautiful day. The ocean was calm nearly all day & the mercury stood at fifty. Mother was so charmed with the placid sea & warm air that she had the boat launched, & Pip rowed her over to Smuttynose & back again. Mother was highly delighted with the excursion; the fresh air & change of scene were very agreeable to her. Last Wednesday the wind came round to the N.W. & the atmosphere became cooler at once. It seems to me, if it were not for the northwest winds, the weather would always be warm.

Bocky has finished his electrical machine. It works splendidly, & *shocks* all individuals who touch it. Bocky took it in the kitchen last night & he tried several experiments, & its action was perfectly satisfactory. The electrical sparks were quite brilliant. . . .

Ever lovingly,
Cedy

* * *January 25, 1862* * *

My Dear & Much Beloved Sister,

. . . The wind has been blowing from the N.E. for ten days, & during that time an immense amount of snow has fallen. The island is covered, buried, submerged, & gone with it, & our good spirits are gone too. Everything seems to have gone wrong lately. Last Friday one of our best cows fell down upon the ice & was hurt so much that we were forced to kill her. Soon after, while we were giving some beets (cut up) to the sheep, one of them attempted to swallow a piece without masticating & choked to death, in a few seconds, before our very eyes. "Well," said Bocky at the time of this catastrophe, "the Fates are against us." Today the wind is blowing a perfect hurricane from the N.E., the same old quarter. We ought to thank our stars that rain, not snow, comes with it. It will fill our little tank & carry off some of this confounded snow at the same time. But this is really a very great storm. It strikes me that I never saw waves of more stupendous size than those which are rushing so furiously into Broad Cove at the present time. They loom like vast moving mountains. . . .

Sunday, January 26. The storm is over, & the ocean is again comparatively calm. The wind changed sometime in the night to the west, & the sea fell rapidly as a natural consequence. But didn't it rain last night! Once more we have a slight peep at the rocks & bushes, & here & there there are small patches of bare ground to be seen. I never saw the swamp[1] so full of water as it is at the present time. If it freezes over smooth we shall have some capital skating. Have you skated any this winter?

Just as soon as we had finished breakfast, Bocky & I went up on the hill,[2] & there were the three vessels riding safely at their moorings. So the mail has not gone in yet—it must be some time since you heard news from the island. Bocky has been hard at work on something which he calls a Dutch clock. As I never saw a regular Dutch clock, I can't say as to whether it looks like one or not. At any rate it is very pretty & will be prettier when completed. I believe the wind is blowing from the N.W. now, by the way it howls round the windows & corners. No communication with the mainland for another week, I suppose. Tonight

Father finished the *Pickwick Papers*, & so Bocky & I are up in our room. Bocky is writing close by, & I have just been joking with him about the positions we assume while writing. Sometimes our noses almost touch the paper. What a funny book *Pickwick* is, isn't it? We all have laughed over it immensely. The fat boy was a very peculiar character. And the scene where Mr. Weller, Sr. gives Mr. Pickwick his money is at once affecting and laugh provoking. . . .

Monday, January 27. . . . Bocky & I have been at work in the new building all day. I finished flooring the rooms, & Bocky planed an immense number of window bands. That *shocking* electrical machine works wonderfully tonight; it always does when the wind is N.W. Bocky has taken several shocks, & says it is very invigorating. I don't fancy the sensation much. Father is reading *Orley Farm* to Mother, down in the kitchen, & Foote[3] is up here in our room attentively perusing an old & well thumbed spelling book. *Orley Farm* is by Anthony Trollope, I believe. . . .

Ever Aff.,
Cedy

1. the swamp: The valley which cuts across from Babb's Cove to Broad Cove is swampy in wet seasons, and at its west end it provided the Laightons with a good skating pond in winter.

2. the hill: The fact that Appledore has two parallel valleys implies three hills or ridges. But when Cedric writes "the hill," he usually means the high elevation to the south of the central valley. Star and the other islands bordering Gosport Harbor were not visible from the hotel; therefore the Laightons must climb the hill to learn about conditions in "the roads."

3. Foote: Pip (Edwin Foote Caswell).

* * February 8, 1862 * *

Dear Sister,

. . . Bocky has been experimenting with hydrogen gas lately. The other evening he got a glass bottle for a retort, and a bladder to hold the gas, and went to work in the most earnest manner. He was successful in separating the gases, and soon had the bladder full of hydrogen. He was so delighted that he hardly knew what to do with it, but he finally concluded to see whether it would ignite. So he cautiously applied the aperture to a light. It no sooner came in contact than our ears were greeted with a loud and unexpected explosion. For a fleeting instant I saw Bocky recoil in astonishment; then we both burst out into a hearty laugh. This was up in our room, and Mother happened to be in her room, which is just under ours, you know. She was, of course, greatly frightened at first, but our laughter reassured her. It is needless to say that the bladder was *smashed*. The next evening he was more successful, and tried several very interesting experiments. Soap-bubbles filled with hydrogen were thrown into the air, and upon applying a light to them they would explode very prettily. We carried the apparatus down into the kitchen, and performed some experiments which pleased Mother very much. One was to hold a bottle over a burning jet of hydrogen, and a very singular noise would be produced. The sound was deep and resonant, and seemed to fill every nook and corner of the old kitchen, and our ears too. The parrot didn't seem to be much edified by the strange music, and the ducks in the cellar gave sundry long drawn quacks of disapprobation. Mother took great delight in igniting the bubbles, and it was very funny to see her draw back and give a deep sigh as she touched them off.

The new building is progressing, though rather slowly. The floors are all laid, except in the big parlor, and the windows are all finished, but there is yet much to be done. There are sinks to make and doors and blinds to hang. Amos Jenness, the joiner, came back last Tuesday.

Father and Mother say, "Tell dear Sister we should be delighted to have her come," and you know that nothing would please your brothers more than a sight of their dear old sister. Mr. Folsom speaks of coming too. It would be nice to have you both come at once. The wretched state of the communication is the only obstacle, and I trust that is not insurmountable.

Love from all to all.

Ever aff.,
Cedy

* * *May 4, 1862* * *

Dear Sister,

. . . Nothing of importance has happened since your departure. The masons have finished their job & have gone; they were six days putting the mortar on. Bocky & I spent Monday, Tuesday, & Wednesday in cleaning the woodwork & floors where the mortar had been dropped, & nice fun we had of it. Amos Jenness, who was at work on the stair rails at the same time, would listen to the scraping of our knives & cloths, and sing out, "Scratch, you devils, scratch!"

. . . The island is covered with spring birds, among which is a little warbler that I always welcome as the sweetest singer of the whole feathered tribe. He stays down by the swamp & sings deliciously. The first swallows came today. I noticed also a meadow chicken & a wild pigeon.

The lovely Bridget & Mary[1] picked a huge mass of dandelions. Beets, cabbages, & lettuce are up in the garden, & the grass & clover seeds that we planted are coming up finely. This forenoon I got four anemones & a dog-tooth violet. Mother was greatly pleased with them, as they are the first of the season. Mother has been rather unwell lately, with a confounded headache, but she is much better today & is in good spirits. Father is very well. Bocky, who is sitting close by, is reading a little piece of poetry beginning, "O sweet new year delaying long," which he seems to admire much. He keeps saying how pretty Sister looked going to Portsmouth in that old whale-boat. . . .

Mother, Father, & Bocky join me in sending loads of love to you & yours.

Affectionately,
Cedy

1. Bridget and Mary: Two of the kitchen help, otherwise unidentified. Probably Mary is the Mary White mentioned in another letter of the same year. Bridget appears frequently from here on, usually with a wry comment on her appearance, behavior, or skill.

* * *May 6, 1862* * *

Dear Sister,

... Mother's slips are getting along finely—many of them have taken root. She is very bright & happy now. This morning she took a row over to Smutty, which did her good. Mr. Folsom's letter came safely & she was much pleased with it.

Tam Tam Tam is bringing coal from Portsmouth; he has made two trips & has got to make two more, so this is the time to send letters. We get the mail pretty often too. The war intelligence seems to be very favorable just now.

Bocky & I have been quite busy today removing the rocks & seaweed which the storm threw over the bank of the upper cove last fall. . . .

I gave the folks a riddle tonight which made them laugh. This is it—Why is a piano like an onion? Give it up? Because it smell odious (melodious).

May 7. . . . We were all delighted to hear of the success of your poem. Mother was sorry the letter did not arrive while you were here, so she could have heard it. Don't forget your wretched brothers in your exalted position. . . .

Aff.,
Cedy

* * *May 18, 1862* * *

Dear Sister,

... Tomorrow we expect one of the Dover & Boston packets with a lot of furniture—bedsteads &c. from Hodge, you know. Well, the packet will go directly to Boston, & Bocky intends to take passage in her so he can tell you about the chair nicely. Bocky has got lots of things to get, & he is going to ship them on board of the packet & come down with them. . . .

Crows have long since ceased to fly over the island, & sheldrakes have gone to the colder regions of the north. We see a stray loon sometimes & now & then a gull, but the time for wild fowl is nearly gone. We are happy to hear of the success of your plumes. Would a yellow-hammer's[1] breast be large enough for a plume?

We have been quite busy painting the new house lately. Over half of it is finished. Mr. Sawyer is still with us & is improving very fast. He is a great billiard player, & it takes the combined skill of the island to beat him. I carried him out fishing the other day, & it did my heart good to see him haul in the *fish*. He caught two while I was catching twenty. . . .

Various things have happened since morning, the most important of which was the arrival of our dear Partner.[2] He is hearty & jolly as can be. He embraced us & said, "This is too good." You can't think how pleased we are to see him. It brings vividly to mind winter before last, which was the most gorgeous winter I ever passed. . . .

Ever aff.,
Cedy

Do send the poem.

1. yellow-hammer: The flicker, or golden winged woodpecker.
2. Partner: Sidney Manley, the Laightons' companion during the winter of 1860-61.

* * *November 9, 1862* * *

Dear Sister,

... The new piazza is progressing slowly. The bottom framework is made & in its place & planked. I suppose it will take a fortnight or more to finish it. But it will be an immense improvement when it is done. There are two joiners at work on it, one of whom is the most indomitable gunner that I ever saw. He don't go gunning week days, but spends all day Sunday in pursuit of some poor old crippled coot, & is happy. He is a small man with a big nose, & enjoys any sort of fun with as much zest as any child. Last Sunday he came into our room at three o'clock in the morning, & mildly requested us to get up & go down to Duck Island with him. This morning (Sunday) he went over on the rocks & sat there with his long gun for two hours while rain was descending in torrents & of course wetting him to the skin. ...

Bocky has been at work out in the shop all day today. That shop is a perfect blessing to him; he seems to enjoy himself immensely out there. He has been making castings of brass today. ...

Yours affectionately,
Cedy

* * *November 23, 1862* * *

Dear Sister,

Your long and pleasant letter beginning Nov. 7th was received a short time since with great delight by the whole family. The box arrived a short time after the letter, but the plants were all frozen. Horrible fact! Tam Tam was very much pleased with his present, and it is related that the tears of supreme pleasure and joy streamed over the countenance of his better half, upon opening and examining the various articles.

Poor Mother has had quite an ill time since I last wrote to you. She was confined to her bed and room for nearly a week. The trouble was that terrible neuralgia; her face was very much swollen and must have been very painful, but she has now quite recovered and is as smiling and pleasant as ever. You can't think how we missed the dear old lady while she was absent from the kitchen.

Aunt Maria was unexpectedly called home a short time ago, but Lizzie is still with us. The new piazza is slowly progressing towards completion. Last week was so exceedingly unpleasant that outdoor work came to a standstill; but today, though cold, has proved a tolerably good working day, and we raised eighty or ninety feet of the frame. We have been raising in sections, you know, and we board and shingle one section before we raise another. . . .

I think your dream was very funny. Of course a fish cannot drown in shallow water. Not that I insinuate that dear Bocky is a fish, but I mean that he can swim faster than the noble sculpin. Many times have I dreamed the same dream of Bocky and you, too, and I have started from my sleep with a shudder, and found to my inexpressible relief that it was only a dream—a dream that for the moment was almost as terrible as the reality. . . .

Yours aff.,
Cedy

* * *December 23, 1862* * *

Dear Sister,

As Tom is going to Portsmouth tomorrow, I thought I would write tonight, though I believe Bocky has got a letter for you to send. It seems that Tam Tam, brimming with gratitude for the bundle of clothes you sent has determined to send you a number of fresh fish. He is going out fishing tomorrow, and will bring the fish over here, which we will pack for him, and he will take them in immediately, so you will be sure to get them nice & fresh. Mother has a few things which she is going to put into Tam's box. Your present of the clothes has made Tam & family happy for the winter. Whenever Tam's wife looks at any of the articles, she exclaims, "God bless her, God bless her." I have seen a good many photographs, ambrotypes, &c., but never in my life did I see anything so perfect as that likeness of Mr. Thaxter. Mother is perfectly delighted with it, & also with Mr. Weiss',[1] and thanks them a thousand times. I don't think the likeness of Mr. Weiss is good, though there was resemblance enough to recall to mind the scene where he & Jonas were shooting peas from an old gun-barrel tied onto a framework of wood, at Mr. Thaxter, who was trying to paper a room. The missiles were aimed through the open window & about every shot took effect. Well do I remember the expression of countenance with which Mr. T. rushed to the window & told them to desist.

Mother has given me a long message for you about birds, but I believe I have forgotten it all. She wishes to know how the robin is, & the canaries. Her canaries look finely, & sing all day long. . . .

Sunday. . . Mrs. Clark came over with Tom bringing the mail, which gave us the particulars of that horrible affair at Fredericksburg. We saw the name of Sidney Willard among the killed, also several other people whom we knew.

We have been making huge preparations for Christmas. We have killed two fat turkeys, and Mother has made immense quantities of pies & goodies. Yesterday Bocky & I went over to Duck Island, where we succeeded in shooting two large ducks, whereat Mother was very much pleased, & pronounced them better than turkeys. . . . Father & Mother are going to make Tam a present of a splendid Christmas dinner for his kindness in getting the mail. . . .

The piazza is finished and a vast improvement it is, both in appearance & comfort. Bocky is making a new shell borer. I guess it will be an elaborate affair, if one can judge by the patterns of wheels &c. which he is going to have cast in iron. It is to go with a treadle.

How is the perfidious hobgoblin? I think that is the funniest expression of wrath that dear little John could have uttered. Mother told Lony one time that he wouldn't see his Dom long, and said he, "Well, if you are going up I'll hold onto your feet."

Father is better & sends love to all. Mother & Bocky join me in sending loads of love.

Yours aff.,
Cedy

1. Mr. Weiss: Rev. John Weiss (1818-79), Levi Thaxter's friend who officiated at the Thaxter wedding in 1851. Ever since Thaxter had introduced Weiss to the Laightons at White Island in 1846, the young clergyman had

considered himself an unofficial member of the Laighton family, and his affection had been returned in kind. He was noted for irrepressible spirits. Weiss served pastorates in Watertown and New Bedford, Mass., but after 1859 he devoted himself to writing at his home in Milton.

* * March 12, 1863 * *

Dear Sister,

. . . The weather has been so tempestuous for a fortnight past our communication with the United States, that were, has been much interrupted. Yesterday was the only respectable day we have had lately, & Tam took advantage of it to row to Portsmouth. I saw his boat going by just at dinner time, deeply laden with fish. Poor Tammy has to struggle against many adverse winds, & as his boat is small it cannot be very pleasant. The last time he came out from P. there came a squall from the N.W. which caught him about half way. The wind blew with terrific violence. I went up in No. 20 to spy for him, but the boat had disappeared. Bocky & I went over to Blue Beach & watched the boiling sea in search of the boat, which we soon had the pleasure of beholding about a mile to windward. We could see it rise on a wave every now & then, & then sink down again, while the spray rose in wreaths around it. Luckily poor Tam was dead to windward, & we soon had the satisfaction of greeting him in Babb's Cove, where the white-capped waves delivered him. His boat was nearly full of water, though he had been bailing all the time. He had lost an oar, too, but he was in excellent spirits & declared that he wasn't born to be drowned. . . .

Last Tuesday was town meeting day[1] at Gosport, when votes were *hove* with great force & certainty. John C. Randall was moderator, & it is reported that he was greatly under the influence of ardent spirits at the time. Origen Caswell[2] (black Republican) was chosen as representative of the mighty city of Gosport. . . .

Please remember us kindly to Mr. T. Bocky blesses him every time he uses the crucible. How is that horse? Mother has read several fearful accidents in regard to hosses. Is he a gentle hoss, & fast? . . .

Hoping that this letter will find you all well & hearty, I am,
Affectionately,
Cedy

1. town meeting day: All actions taken at this meeting were nullified, and another meeting was called for August 11 to transact the annual business. See the Gosport Town Records as published in the *New England Historical and Genealogical Register*, LXVIII (April, 1914), 137.

2. Origen Caswell: Origen Smith Caswell was the youngest son of "old Joe," and a brother of Lemuel B., Joseph A., Andrew J., and numerous sisters. Origen, born March 17, 1840, became the proprietor of the Gosport House.

* * *June 14, 1863* * *

Dear Sister,

... Bocky has recovered from the sickly effect of *Bosting* air, & is once more the healthy Appledorean. I showed him your note in which you described the party, & the poor boy heaved a long & lugubrious sigh.

We have been wickedly at work all day (Sunday) launching & ballasting boats, beside carrying up two & a half tons of coal which arrived yesterday evening. We have to keep pretty busy now, for in six days the *Sibyl*[1] will commence to run, & we have got to shear the sheep, get four or five moorings off, & mow all the grass at Smuttynose previously to the advent of *boarding time.* The island looks bravely now—plenty of wild flowers & a bright coat of green—a little more encouraging than it looked last March.

This afternoon I went over to Duck Island in search of gulls' eggs, but there were none. The medrake or swallow-tailed gull is the only variety that breeds at the island, and every year the eggs are taken by the fishermen; so the poor things are getting shy. I don't think they will build here this season, but if they do I will be sure to get some eggs. . . .

Trusting you will excuse bad spelling, bad punctuation, & bad writing, I remain, truly & lovingly,

Cedy

1. The Laightons were still having their problems with Capt. Preble. Oscar, writing to Celia on May 3, 1863, says:

> Cedy and I went in to New Castle yesterday after dinner to see the lofty owner of the "Sibyl," in order to make arrangements for our regular packet. I never heard any man talk so pompously as Preble in my life. It was horrid to listen to him. We all jumped into the "Sibyl" together with the angel, John Amazeen, who lent you his coat once. The poor man has lost 5 children since last summer. We got home at

five o'clock, but father could come to no definite understanding with Preble. He is a most vexatious man. I only wish John Amazeen owned the boat.

* * September 26, 1863 * *

Dear Sister,

I owe you a hundred thousand thanks for your encouraging letter of the eighteenth. The miserable little note that I sent the other day has told you that we have not forgotten you, "O Island Rose"![1] On the contrary, we have thought many times of your "regal eye" & "kingly brow." You speak of the September gale. I guess they are pretty frequent, for all day today the wind has been howling from the northward with the greatest fury. Notwithstanding the storm, Bocky & I took the new wherry & went off by the *Sibyl*'s moorings mackerel fishing. We caught about two hundred good ones. . . . Tam Tam has got into another row with his neighbor, Mrs. Clark, & he came over here yesterday, saying, "Mr. Laighton, if Ma'am Clark doesn't leave Smuttynose, I shall." Upon which Father said, "Depart, Tom, depart." So Tam went away. . . .

O my dearest Sister, I am so pleased to see that you really wish me to come up, that you would be glad to see me, & I am so sorry to think that I cannot come. *Next* fall I shall have more time. We expect the lumber for the cottage[2] every day; as soon as that is taken care of, Bocky is going to Boston for a day or two, I believe. Mother is going to Portsmouth, as soon as the Burnets go, to stop a week or two. Mother gave me a long message about caps, birds, & flowers, but I believe I have forgotten it all. Poll, the demon parrot, got out today & to wing. The wind blew her smash into a clump of bushes, where she was caught by Bocky, who, knowing the fiendish nature of the bird, enveloped his hands in a stout cloth, & so was not crippled for life. During the whole operation, Dom stood in the wash-house doorway, calmly contemplating the scene.

The cottage work goes on rapidly, the cellar is most finished, & by the time the lumber gets here the foundation will be ready for the frame. I wish you could see the sweet peas up by the billiard room; there are hundreds of blossoms now. You should have seen the expression of Father's countenance when he heard what you said about Mother going to Newtonville. It implied great disgust; he says he cannot let her go to P., even. Mother, Father, & Bocky send loads of love to you all. . . . And now, O Island Rose, good night & pleasant dreams.

Everlastingly,
Cedy

1. "O Island Rose": An anonymous note on the back of the original letter tells us that "O Island Rose," "regal eye," and "kingly brow" are probably quoted from a poem by Marie Mason, wife of Lowell Mason. The poem has not been located.

2. the cottage: During this autumn and winter, the Laightons built a new house for Thomas and Eliza on the slope northwest of the hotel, facing south and overlooking the front lawn of the Appledore House. The building was to be famous later as the Celia Thaxter Cottage.

*   *   November 15, 1863   *   *

Dear Sister,

. . . We have been very busy with the new house, and have got the upper story plastered. If it continues warm for about ten days, the lower story will be plastered, but a cold snap will delay it until the spring. Last Sunday Bocky and I took the *Lone Star* (Jonsen's little schooner) and went to Portsmouth. The wind was northeast, and just as we reached the wharf it commenced to rain; so we fastened our boat and rushed up to the Rockingham House, where we made ourselves miserable for a whole afternoon. Next morning was fine, so we got through with our business as early as possible and arrived here at dinner time.

Before we started we went to the express office and got the box which you sent. Mother was greatly delighted with her caps and rose water. She says, "Thank the dear child a thousand times." She sends loads of love to all. Tam Tam has moved to Portsmouth, so he knows naught of the contents of the box. . . .

Did I tell you about the wreck of the *Spray*? The *Spray* was our whale-boat, you know, and was worth a hundred and fifty dollars. The mooring broke in the night, and a fierce northwester hurled the poor little craft upon the rocks.

This has been a stormy day. The rain has been falling in torrents, and the wind has been howling from the southeast at a great rate. Notwithstanding the inclemency of the weather, Charley, the indomitable gunner, was up long before daylight and out upon the hills. He returned at breakfast time without any game and drenched to the skin. After breakfast he sat in the backdoor way shooting rats, and while he was thus occupied, Bocky got an old stuffed henhawk, which we happened to have on the premises, and placed it on the wall by Blue Beach. He then took a cod-line and fastened one end to the bird, and went off with the other end to a safe distance. Soon one of the joiners came rushing up to the door where Charley was and said, "Quick, Charley, there's a large fish-hawk on the wall!" So poor innocent Charley, the victim of this fiendish plot, ran out in the greatest excitement imaginable. All the joiners were in the joke, and they stood on the piazza watching him. He crept warily down to the boat-house, and taking *deadly* aim he fired. Bocky, who was still behind the wall, heard the report, and he gave the string a pull and over went the hawk; he then crept quickly up to where the bird fell, and just as Charley was clambering over the wall to pick up his game, he arose like a ghost in the very place where the bird fell. Charley was perfectly astounded, and for a few moments he said not a word, but stood gazing at Bocky, while every lineament of his countenance expressed extreme surprise and some terror. Pretty soon, however, the shouts of laughter from the piazza told him plainly that he was badly sold; so he came down to the house and for a time was rather melancholy, but in the afternoon he was fortunate enough to shoot a heron, and his spirits rose again.

Mother has been very busy lately with all the workmen to cook for. Tomorrow three of them are going off. Mother has nobody with her except "Gimmy come good death"[1] and Julia[2] of the rueful countenance, whom you doubtless remember. . . .

Ever aff.,
Cedy

1. "Gimmy come good death": From this point on there are frequent references to one of the kitchen girls as "Grim death," "Grimmy death," "Gasping death," or "Gimmy" in various combinations. I suspect she is Bridget.
2. Julia: Probably the same girl as she whom Cedric calls "Julia Somebody, . . . a daughter of the Emerald Isle" in the letter of January 1, 1865. See p. 81.

* * *November 29, 1863* * *

Dear Sister,

The communication between this "island home" & the continent seems to have come to a standstill, for it is now nineteen days since we got the mail. . . . Last Monday the masons finished the plastering, & together with the two joiners took the *Ripple* & rowed to Rye. The joiners are coming back tomorrow or next day to finish the new house, for though the plastering is finished, the window & door frames are to be cased, door hung, stairs made, & lots to be done in the joinering line. Bocky & I, at present, are engaged framing a building which we intend to have for a billiard room. It is to be placed against the side of this old house & is to be connected with the bar-room, thus bringing billiard room & bar under the direction of one person. The old billiard room is to be made into sleeping rooms. We are also going to enlarge the office, & make extensive alterations in the kitchen & dining room, so we shall probably be very busy until the boat commences to run. Father will probably move into the new house about the middle of March. The weather has been so mild since the plastering was finished that it is now out of danger of freezing, which is extremely lucky.

Mother has been reading all day, and Bocky & I found the dear old lady crying very heartily over some of the affecting passages.

White owls are very plentiful just now. This morning I saw two sitting on the fence just beyond the swamp. They watch mornings & evenings for rats. The other evening we saw one pounce upon his prey & carry it off to a neighboring ledge, where he *discussed* it at his leisure. . . .

Father, Mother, & Bocky send loads of love to you, as does

Your loving brother,
Cedy

* * *December 13, 1863* * *

Dear Sister,

. . . Bocky has been enjoying a severe cold in the head, but he is much better today, and is searching all the Philosophies, &c.

with the greatest wildness, for a *power*: something that will be cheaper than the steam engine. He walks about the room crying, "Oh if I only had a power," which causes both of us to laugh. This morning when we got up we beheld the first snow of the season; everything was white with it, but now it is raining and the gray rocks are visible again. I saw numerous loons and three sheldrakes in by the slip today. They did not seem to be inclined to laughter. . . .

Well, dear Sister, evening has come upon us, and I haven't finished this letter yet. I tried to this forenoon and had just got to the last word of the last paragraph when I thought I would take a peep out of "No. 32." I went and beheld a large loon close in by the black ledge. I rushed for my gun, and in the space of two or three hours I secured three fine loons. Mother was greatly delighted. Everything at the island is pretty jolly, except that we do not hear from *America* very often.

Good bye, Skipper Grans.[1]

Yours most affectionately,
Cedy

1. Skipper Grans: Star Islanders called grandparents "Grans" and "Gwammy." In subsequent letters, Cedric often calls Celia "Gwammy," and signs himself as "Grans." In this instance, addressing Celia as "Skipper Grans" is a playful variation.

* * *December 28, 1863* * *

Dear Sister,

Johnson has just got down from Boston, & is going to Ports., so I scratch a few lines to let you know that we are alive & kicking. Father has been quite sick lately. He had a severe attack of paralysis or something of the kind. For a time we were very much alarmed, but he is much better today. . . .

Affectionately,
Cedy

* * *January 3, 1864* * *

Dear Sister,

Last Monday I sent a little note to you by Jonsen, and Wednesday the *Village-Maid* brought out the mail and your two good letters of Dec. twenty-first and twenty-second, which caused us all great delight. Dear Father was taken sick about ten days ago, and since that time he has hardly been able to move without assistance, and has not been able to use his right arm and leg. How I do pity him. Think what a life of physical torture he has had to endure, and yet he has struggled manfully with the world, and his great misfortune, and has triumphed. This morning, in trying to get from the bed to his chair, he fell (his limbs refused to support him), but luckily without injury. I think, however, that he improves every day. Every day he grows brighter and more hopeful. I read your letters to Father and Mother, and they both laughed heartily over your account of the children's pranks. Karly's letter was very *rich,* and good too. I should like to hear them repeat their pieces very much.

The last accounts we had, before your last, were that old Pachyderm was sick unto death, and now we find him actually racing with the steam engine. Hurrah for old Thick Skin; we thought that noble *hoss* was dead. What fun it must have been flying along at the topmost speed of your Pegasus. But was it not a little dangerous too? Perhaps and undoubtedly you are very skillful in managing your steed.

Last fall Bocky and I hired a horse and carriage one evening while we were in Portsmouth. When we first went into the stable, the owner of the horses said he was not in the habit of letting horses to strangers, and that all his horses were tired out, &c. But one of our friends happened to come in who introduced us & *backed* us for a thousand dollars, & the horse was instantly forthcoming. We jumped aboard the carriage, Bocky took the helm, and we steered up through Islington Street, and there stopped at the house of a friend. Bocky jumped out of the carriage & went into the house, & I waited outside. While I was waiting, the cars came thundering over a bridge a few rods at one side. The lights in the engine gleamed, the whistle shrieked, and the earth quaked with the rumbling of the wheels. The scene was entirely new to me; I enjoyed it. The horse pricked up his ears, but was otherwise perfectly unconcerned. All the way back Bocky and I were joking each other on our skill in driving. While we were going through Market Street the horse suddenly darted to one side. "There," said Bocky, "he's shied!" Whereupon we both began to laugh immensely. The horse, finding that we were not regarding him very much, slackened his pace & walked along in a doleful way, which did not agree with our ideas of a dashing *turnout.* So Bocky said, "Strike him with the whip." I took the whip and touched the animal very gently, whereupon he flourished his tail in a very indignant manner. "He thinks it is a fly," said Bocky, and the remark tickled us so, that Bocky dropped the reins, and we both fell back in the carriage, overcome with laughter. We laughed till we cried. Meanwhile the horse, doubtless suspecting that we were rather too green to manage him, trotted gallantly back to his stable. . . .

Bocky is out in the shop trying to cast something or other. This morning I persuaded Mother to believe that I was sick, and she gave me a large bottle of elderberry wine. I seized the bottle & rushed upstairs here, made a good fire, and then I filled up my glass and sat down very contentedly and—sipped. As time flew by, I noticed that the bottle was fast becoming empty, and everything about the room wheeled dreamily before my vision. So said I to myself: This wine is very good, and I guess I will write to Sister. And so you see, you dear, here I am.

Yesterday I attempted to saw out some pieces for fish reels, with the circular saw, and in so doing I innocently placed the thumb of my left hand in contact with the fast revolving saw. As you may well imagine, the consequence of this pretty manoeuver was a jagged and extensive gash which will render the hand useless for a week or more. If I have any more of these pleasant little incidents to relate, you will doubtless begin to think that I must present a most doleful and scarred appearance.

Christmas and New Year went by very quietly and pleasantly here. Father succeeded in wishing Mother merry Xmas *first,* by waking her up at midnight. This has been his invariable joke for years, much to Mother's indignation. Santa Claus must have skipped our poor house when he took his annual flight for the chimneys. Though the delicious turkey which we had for dinner might possibly be traced to him, and I think the hearty appetite & fine spirits with which we sat down to it were undoubtedly the gifts of Santa Claus. . . .

Very affectionately,
Cedy

P.S. Your good kind note of Dec. 31st has just arrived. Jonsen brought the mail over just as I was finishing this. We don't think Father's sickness is very serious, and we all hope to see him perfectly well and about again in a few weeks.

Everlastingly thine,
Cedy

* * *January 10, 1864* * *

Dear Sister,

There are two letters on the way to you now; but I write to you this evening because there is nothing else that I can do comfortably. Bocky is flying about the room in about the same manner as a good comfortable maniac would do. I tried to read but it was no use, for the boy kept singing and talking in a dazed sort of way of what he is going to do. I inferred from his remarks that the most important thing on his mind is the cleaning of the chimney of his lamp. This is Sunday evening, you know. Bocky and I have devoted the day to recreation and sport. (That's a nice way of spending Sabbath, isn't it?) Bocky turned a couple of napkin rings and cut up some tissue paper, while I cleaned my gun and washed my face. Bocky is going to make a balloon of the tissue paper. He is sitting by the long table now, and is trying to melt a piece of steel with his blowpipe and a fluid lamp. All the time he keeps screeching, "What a time I'm having!"

Father is getting along very comfortably. Yesterday he did not feel so well, but today he is better than I have yet seen him. Amos and Mace, the two joiners, went away yesterday. Amos will come back sometime about the first of March. Yesterday I shot the white owl, the one that has been on the island for a month or more. The poor bird was complacently pluming himself on the very tip-top of the belfry, and when I fired he came tumbling down upon the dining-room roof, stone dead. The reason that this merciless act was perpetrated was that the owl was strongly suspected of having a hankering for turkey. A short time ago a couple of these minute fowls disappeared, and Mother said, "Shoot the owl," which was accordingly done. The wings are not injured much, so I shall send them to you as soon as I get some other wings to send with them. . . .

I courted ye as much as a year and a half, be dad's house, be dad's roof, and now you won't eat ryecake, corncake, nutcake, pancake, doughcake—and daubcake—and now you've left me for a wood-sawyer.

The above paragraph will probably astonish you, but be not alarmed as it is simply a little piece which Bocky takes great pleasure in repeating for the edification of his family. Before writing this little piece, I feel that I ought to have given you a little preparation, for the quick succession of cakes, I am afraid, will startle you. And the wild beginning of "I courted ye" will cause you to hold up your hands in amazement. However, it is written, and all I can hope for is that the shock on your nerves will not bring on the neuralgia or diphtheria.

I long for the mail to come, for I know there is a letter from you waiting in P.

Everybody sends loads of love to you.

Lovingly,
Cedy

* * *January 17, 1864* * *

Dear Sister,

. . . Last Wednesday Johnson brought out a couple of boxes—one was for me & the other was for Mother. They both contained *caps*. Mother's was from Mrs. Bartlett of Concord, & was a very funny shaped cap, though it was made of very rich materials. Mother took the box into her room, and Bocky & I rushed after her to see it opened. As soon as Mother got the lid off of the box, we grabbed the cap & placed it on her head. It looked so funny that we burst into a fit of laughter in which Father joined most heartily. Mother found that the cap was on wrong, so she turned it upside down, & it looked a little better. My box contained the Scotch cap which Mrs. Hill promised so long ago. Mother thought it rather pretty.

Father's attack of sickness was very sudden, though he had a premonition of it a day or two before it came on so severely. It seems to have left him perfectly well except the numbness in his side & arm. I do not think he suffers any. At least he does not complain, but is as good & cheerful as can be. He had a very slight attack last summer, with the same symptoms, & he thought then that it might be a consequence of using a cane all his life. He has been trying Bocky's galvanic battery, which seems to help his arm slightly.

Bocky has been out in the shop all day. He says he has been enjoying himself immensely blowing glass & working on the balloon. The balloon is a perfect failure and he has given it up in disgust. I believe a glass bubble burst as he was blowing it, & burnt his fingers, which of course was pure enjoyment to him. . . .

Bocky & I are painting the inside of the new house, so as to have it ready for the old folks when warm weather comes on. This morning Mother's little sparrow sung a jubilant spring song. How many weeks it is since we have heard the sparrows sing. As he piped with his clear voice, visions of green fields & blooming flowers seemed to take the place of the dreary snow & ice. Of all the music in the world, give me the notes of the song sparrow.

Last Friday was the pleasantest day of the winter. Bocky & I made a holiday of it, & took our boat & rowed about five miles outside of the islands to the southeast. It was quite calm & pleasant & we enjoyed ourselves much. . . .

Lovingly,
Cedy

*   *   *January 24, 1864*   *   *

Dear Sister,

Your elegantly illuminated letter of the thirteenth arrived last Thursday and also the box containing Mother's silk. Yesterday your good letter to Mother, dated the eighteenth, came much to the joy of the whole family. Mother is very much pleased with the silk, and sends a thousand thanks to you for getting it so nicely. She says she shall not need any more caps, and was very much pleased with your thoughtfulness in suggesting it. Father is getting along very nicely. We all think he improves every day.

Poor dear Sister, what a disagreeable fall you must have had, and all because of that fiend in the shape of a hoss, commonly called Pachyderm. Bocky and I have consumed most of our leisure time in hurling anathemas at the infamous "Kettripid," which could they have reached him would probably have annihilated the varmint. We suggest, as he threw you out of the sleigh in the attempt to get his dinner, that it would be a good notion to mix up a little strychnine with his oats, and let his punishment be death by eating his dinner. Thus he would be effectually cured of rushing off to his meals ere you alight from the carriage.

I believe Bocky has given you some account of the Beebe[1] affair. Later advices have reached us since Bocky wrote, however, and we learn that the highest circles in the fashionable world of Gosport have been thrown into the most intense excitement and amazement by a discovery which is truly enough to make the bones of Hamlet turn a summerset in their coffin. It seems that three years ago, Nett, of the House of Lemmy,[2] suddenly and most mysteriously missed a couple of "webs" of cloth. Those "webs" were recently found in the possession of Mrs. Beebe. When Nett first missed the "webs," she laid the theft at the door of her sister-in-law, the wife of Joseph, and therefore she has not smiled upon the said wife of Joseph for many months. You may now imagine the astonishment of Nett when, in the House of Beebe, and in the august presence of the town clerk,[3] Aunt Sally,[4] and numerous other of the worthy citizens of Gosport, she found, discovered, and recognized the identical webs of cloth. To say that Nett, of the House of Lemmy, was wroth, would be but half expressing it. The House of Beebe was soon a scene of the most disgraceful uproar and confusion. Nett rushed upon Mrs. Beebe and commenced to slap her in the face; the town clerk, unwilling to leave without an honorable scar, rushed at Beebe and slapped him in the face; and Aunt Sally, seeing everyone so pleasantly employed, determined to have her share and so commenced to slap Beebe's baby. After the slapping was over, the trio walked slowly and majestically away from the Parsonage, amid the tears and groans of the House of Beebe. The last accounts from Gosport inform us that Nett has called for a meeting, to be held in the stone church, when a full exposition of the case is to be given to the excited populace.

Dearest Sister, I trust you will excuse this long account of an unpleasant affair, for I thought I could not do better than tell you all the news.

Mother, Father, & Bocky send loads of love to you all. Dom says kiss the children a thousand times for her.

Lovingly,
Cedy

1. Beebe: Rev. George R. Beebe served as minister from 1856 to 1869, his salary paid by the Society for Propagating the Gospel among the Indians and Others in North America. Having had previous medical training, and having been granted a leave of some months in 1860-61 to attend lectures at Harvard Medical School, Beebe was no ordinary clergyman. He said in one of his annual reports: "Indeed, without his knowledge of medicine, incomplete as it is, your missionary could not have exerted half the influence he has been enabled to, nor consistently have remained among them half so long. . . . There are some here who 'would not give a cent for all the

ministers in the world'; nor do they 'care much about teachers'; but 'a doctor is worth something and no mistake.'"

2. Nett of the House of Lemmy: Henrietta, the wife of Lemuel B. Caswell, and mistress of the Atlantic House.

3. town clerk: Perhaps this was Origen Caswell, Nett's brother-in-law, who had been Town Clerk the previous year. In that capacity he had recorded a warrant for a town meeting to be held on Aug. 11, 1863. The purpose of the meeting appears to have been the ratification or modification of action taken illegally in March of that year. (See Cedric's mention of the earlier meeting, p. 52.) There is no record of who was elected Town Clerk on August 11.

4. Aunt Sally: Mother of Lemuel B. Caswell, thus Nett's mother-in-law. Aunt Sally, with her late husband, "old Joe," had kept a boarding house for many years, having entertained Richard Henry Dana, Jr. in 1843. She was famous locally for her apple turnovers.

* * *January 27, 1864* * *

Dear Sister,

. . . Father has been quite bright this pleasant weather. Yesterday he walked across his room without assistance, which was very encouraging. He says that he feels he is getting well, though very slowly. Bocky & I have been *very* busy for a week past trying to finish the outside of the new billiard-room. Today we put on the last shingle, & our joy thereat was expressed in loud shouts & other demonstrations of gratitude. We have painted the whole of the new house, inside. It is a most lovely "lemon" green color, the prettiest shade of green that ever I gazed upon.

The Beebe affair is drawing slowly to a denouement. We heard today that Lemmy solemnly avers if restoration & apology are not immediately made, the "sharp tooth" of the law will descend upon the House of Beebe, & there will be such a slapping as was never heard of in the quiet annals of Gosport. . . .

Lovingly,
Cedy

* * *January 31, 1864* * *

Dear Sister,

. . . The ground is again covered with ice & snow. Cold blasts sweep across the sea from the northeast, & the waves are curling their green edges around the eastern shore. Bocky & I keep our spirits up by repeating as rapidly as possible the following piece:

"Sargent, deou yeou drink?" "Billy, I deou not; I deou not drink even to a glass of good cider." "Well, Mr. Sargent, yeou air a little more temperate than I am, for I will drink a glass of good neuw cider." You will perceive at once that this is a recommendation.

Father is getting along, though very slowly. Mother, who is the best judge, as she is with him constantly, says that she thinks he improves every day. I believe I did not say anything about the cap which you sent with the silk, though I intended to. At any rate, you must know that it arrived safely, as it was packed with the silk.

By this time you must be in the full and happy possession of the facts of the Beebe affair, so it would be useless for me to write anything more about it. I shall just state, however, that B. is totally undisturbed by the scandalous stories which are spreading from Gosport over this little globe of ours. On the contrary, he seems to be uninterested in the vituperative eloquence of Nett, or the threats of Lemmy, & goes about speaking & acting as though he were not personally concerned in the matter.[1]

Gosport, the mighty metropolis of N. H. was lately the scene of an atrocity which has not been equaled since the days of Procrustes or Polyphemus. It seems that old Asa,[2] one of the patriarchs of Gosport, was quietly seated in his room the other evening, when in rushed Jim Haley,[3] who immediately began to whop the patriarch till his cries, at Cape Ann even, resounded loud & clear, & summoned the entire population of Gosport to the rescue. . . .

All send love to you & all the family.

Sincerely,
Cedy

1. not personally concerned in the matter: Perhaps he had too much on his mind. His routine activities, as outlined in an annual report to the Society, were as follows:

> Retires at ten O'clock, rises at six. . . . About fifty nights in the year this rest is broken by calls of the sick, made upon him in his medical capacity. Breakfast at eight, the two hours previous, after rising, being spent in private devotion, reading the Greek Testament and other biblical studies; after breakfast, family devotions. At nine o'clock the round of the sick is made, there being commonly from three to twenty on his list as a physician; then reading and study and dinner occupy the time till two o'clock P.M., and the remainder of

the afternoon is devoted to pastoral visits: the missionary aiming to have direct religious conversation with everyone over seven years of age at least once a month. The evenings . . . are spent in preparations for the Sabbath and other studies. Amid these regular duties your missionary picks out time for a multitude of small jobs, such as putting on a new shingle; fastening a loose clapboard; setting a pane of glass; mending a lock or hinge, either on the church or the parsonage or the school-house; sawing his own wood; bringing his stores from the boat; sweeping the church; making the fires; and ringing the bell. Then his duties as chairman of the Selectmen and of the School Committee come in for a portion of his time; also attention to visitors.

Beebe made some generous estimates of the population he might be called upon to serve: permanent inhabitants, 200; seamen and fishermen, 1500; visitors, 10,000.

2. old Asa: Asa Caswell, one of Star Island's crustier characters, a brother of "old Lem" and "old Joe," was born January 8, 1805. He figures in two anecdotes related by Oscar in *Ninety Years*.

3. Jim Haley: James Haley, about thirty years old at this time, was a Gosport fisherman.

* * *February 7, 1864* * *

Dear Sister,

. . . Father progresses very slowly. Some days he feels quite bright & on others he seems to be perfectly miserable. Tonight he is quite unwell. He has not been able to use his right arm at all yet. Mother is with him all the time nearly. I trust & hope to see him about soon, but I am afraid it will be a long time before he is able to leave his room. . . .

Everything seems to be very weird nowadays. I have come to the conclusion that I am a little "foolish." The other day I got eight fresh fish of Jansen, & as I scraped the scales from their shining sides, I exclaimed, "Hullo, you shiny, scaly old haddicks; what news do you bring from the salt sea?"[1]

I have been reading *The Wayside Inn* today, & I am perfectly delighted with it. Mother is reading aloud to Father that "unique, original, purely American novel, *Round the Block*." Both books Bocky got when he was at Ports. . . .

The whole Laighton family refuse to listen to the preposterous idea of your giving up your visit. It must not be. If you do not come in March I shall drink a pint of blood.

I do not expect to be able to leave the island this winter, but Bocky will probably visit Boston in the course of a month.

All send love to you.

Affectionately,
Cedy

1. "Hullo, etc.": Almost three years before, on March 10, 1861, Celia had written Oscar:

> I wish you could have seen me set Maria into fits of laughter the other day, quite unintentionally, by addressing a fish I was cutting up in the kitchen. I didn't think anybody was listening. "Blessed old haddock," quoth I, "with your lilac skin all striped with black and your lovely old intelligent countenance, can't you tell me the last news from the salt sea, or did you leave it too long ago?" Whereat the handmaiden collapsed and I subsided from musing aloud to musing in silence.

* * February 14, 1864 * *

Dear old Skipper Gwammy Grans,

I wonder how you are, & what you are up to today. Bocky & I are wheezing & sneezing & puffing & shrieking with incipient *diphtheria,* or cold in the head, which seems to be quite the fashion at Appledore this winter. Dear Father has really seemed much better lately, especially yesterday & today. Last week he took some lobelia & was apparently much benefited by it. He sleeps pretty well & has an excellent appetite. . . .

Gosport seems to be pretty quiet at the present time; at least we hear nothing extraordinary from that quarter. Whether Mrs. B. has returned the stolen goods, or whether the wrathful Mrs. C. has held any more meetings or has introduced the sharp tooth of the law, I am unable to say. It is probable, though, that the calm & unconcerned demeanor of Mr. B. will have due effect upon the irate Gosportians, &, in my humble opinion, the time is not far distant when peace & quietness will again reign among the upper ten thousand of the city. It is to be hoped that the slapping will have a beneficial effect upon the citizens in general & the Beebe family in particular.

It is said that Jim Haley was very much intoxicated when he committed the assault upon old Asa, & I suppose he took that method to express the exceeding joviality of his mind. I guess old Asa hardly saw the *goak!* . . .

"Black lie the hills, swiftly doth daylight flee"; therefore I must bring this poor note to an end. O regal eye!! . . .

Father, Mother, and Bocky join me in sending love to all.

                                 Affectionately,
                                 Cedy

                        *   * *February 21, 1864* * *

Dear Sister,

Jansen came out yesterday, but much to our disappointment he brought no mail. It seems that Amos Jenness, the joiner, who arrived here day before yesterday, took the mail out of the office just before starting from P. Amos had been partaking extensively of the curse of humanity, & of course he laid the mail-bag down somewhere & forgot to take it up again. Jansen is going in tomorrow or next day, so he will try to hunt it up. It was a wretched piece of business to lose the mail, as we have not heard from the land for a week, & there must have been a letter from you. . . .

Wednesday "the storm came down" in the shape of a northwester. Of all the blowing that ever I experienced, Skipper Gwammy, that was the master!! The house was swaying perceptibly to & fro in the blast, the windows were rattling, & everything was in a state of confusion. I rushed for the therm & found the mercury stationary at 10° above zero, a temperature which Bayard Taylor speaks of in his Arctic reminiscences as uncomfortably warm. If such is the case, I say come good death. Bocky & I passed the forenoon in bottling cider. We filled three hundred and ten bottles. In the afternoon we made three barrels of good soap and then put on numerous coats, comforters, & mittens, & went over on the hills to look up the lambs. We found most of them well & frisky, & drove them all up in the cellar. Three little fellows that were nearly frozen we took in by the kitchen fire. The wind blew so furiously that we found it difficult to maintain an erect posture. The western shore was deluged in freezing spray. An immense wave would strike Little Island & send the foam high in the air & the wind would carry it to John Smith's monument[1] & beyond. . . .

Thursday the wind still continued to blow, & the glass indicated one degree below zero, what Bayard Taylor would pronounce warm & summer-like. . . . On going out to the barn, we found a calf (born in the night) frozen stiff. . . .

Saturday the wind was still from the N.W., though quite moderate. Jansen came out, as I said before, & we went over to Smutty; got some meal, potatoes, & eggs which he brought out. You may imagine that the eggs & potatoes were *slightly* frozen. Father was much better that day. He tried Bocky's battery in the evening, & his arm was much benefited thereby. Mother also tried the battery for her neuralgia, & the way she shrieked was a caution to the uninitiated. Father & Bocky & I laughed at her. . . .

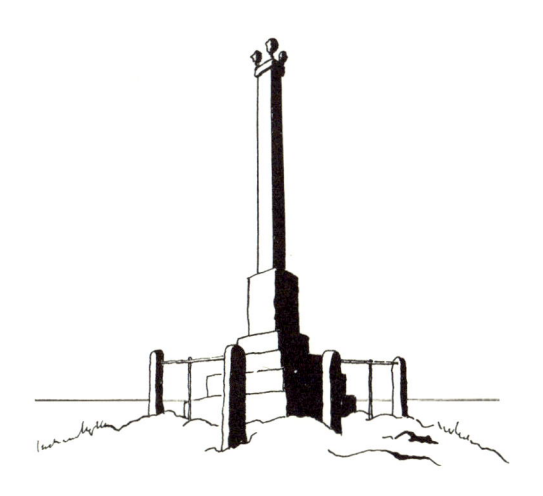

All the news that we have heard from the Gosportian parson & family is this. Mr. B. is superintending the erection of a monument to the memory of John Smith. It is to have numerous inscriptions, & is to be placed on Star Island.[2] Mrs. B. bought a stove for the schoolhouse with the school funds, & immediately took it into her own house & has been using it ever since, & means to keep it, I cal'late. . . .

Well, dear old Skipper Gwammy, this letter is getting rather long, & long letters are not good, unless one can write as pleasantly as you do. . . .

With much love, most affectionately,

Cedy

1. John Smith's monument: On the crest of Appledore's "big hill" there was formerly a cairn which was reputed to have been built by John Smith's men in 1614. In 1908 the U. S. Government bought the top of the hill for a Coast Guard station, and used the stones of the cairn in the foundations of the building. In this passage Cedric is referring to the cairn, although in the same letter he speaks of another "John Smith's monument" planned for Star Island.

2. to be placed on Star Island: The monument erected under Mr. Beebe's direction was only in part the one standing today. The original had a tall triangular shaft, and at each of the three top corners was the carved head of a Turkish soldier. These heads commemorated the successive decapitation of three opponents whom Smith met in single combat when he was fighting in central Europe against the infidels. The Turks' heads adorned his coat of arms and appear on his gravestone in London.

Eventually this wooden column blew down, and in 1914 was replaced by a solid granite block with a bronze tablet.

* * *February 28, 1864* * *

Dear Sister,

. . . Bocky went to Ports. Friday & returned last night at eleven o'clock. The wind blew heavily from the N.W., so the boat that he came out in anchored by Broad Cove. He brought out three or four stoves, carpeting, lumber, &c., so we were up about all night taking care of things. The things, as you will of course understand, are for the new house, which we are getting ready for occupancy as fast as possible. We have been putting down carpets today, though it's Sunday. Father begins to long for a change of scene, so he will move up to the new house sometime in the course of the next week if the weather is good & he feels equal to it.

Wednesday we wheeled him out on the piazza, as the day was mild & pleasant. That was the first time he had been out of his room for nine weeks & two days! . . .

Dear old Skipper Gwammy Grans, what a good time you are having, to be sure. If you only had somebody in the kitchen that you could depend on, but alas! that pinnacle of delight has never been reached by any American family. While Mother was sick we were left to the mercy of *Grim Death*. You can imagine our woe. I meant to tell you in this letter that Father and Mother are comparatively well at present, but hardly know whether I have done it or not. They both send loads of love to you all, & so does Bocky. Hurrah for the pome on the Salt Sea!

         Lovingly,
         Cedy

* * March 6, 1864 * *

Dear Sister,

I have been longing to grab this old Gillott pen all day but have been so busy that my spirit has nearly departed from my body. Bocky & I are all alone in the big house here, & the wind is howling & the rain is dripping with great violence this evening. The cottage home is brilliantly illumined & looks quite strange & pretty, & the old folks seem quite happy & I think much improved in health, though Father's hand & arm do not gain so fast as we could wish. Last Thursday was the day that they moved up, & the day dawned upon a pretty sick party of Appledoreans. Father had his old trouble; Mother had a terrible pain in her side; Bocky had a lame back & I had a stiff neck, so the groans & curses were loud & deep. Notwithstanding all these difficulties the moving was accomplished without loss of a human life, though a leg was broken—the leg of Father's easy-chair.

Bocky & I had to put down some boards from the cottage home to the big piazza to wheel the chair on, & when we got halfway up, one of the casters came off & the leg was smashed, but we managed to propel the *kerridge* on three wheels safely, and Father was sitting in the N.W. room of the cottage home, with a cheerful fire, precisely at two bells (big bell on top of house & dinner bell) (Goak!) waiting for Mother. Mother was so unwell that walking any distance seemed a tremendous exertion to her, so Bocky & I racked our feeble brains for a conveyance. After a few moments a brilliant thought struck Boc. & he rushed for—what do you imagine? Not the resplendent vehicle that is harnessed up behind miserable old Pachyderm every Sunday, but—ah! Weep, Limb of an ancient and honorable family tree, for it was a wheelbarrow!!!! Though the instrument was insignificant & humble, the end attained was great, for Mother was carried with ease & rapidity, &, notwithstanding her illness, was laughing all the way up to the new house. I am so tired that I shall have to give up the idea of finishing this tonight, so I will bid you good night. "When through wild March the throstle calls.". . .

        Yours aff. but deathly,
        Grans

* * *March 20, 1864* * *

Dear Grans,

My God of Heavens, tell me not that old Pachy is to be sold! Tam Tam brought your good letter of March eleventh yesterday, much to our delight. What made you commence by scolding me when I have *writ* every Sunday this winter? . . . Oh grimmy death, that poor old pachydermatous kettriped! To think that after faithfully performing his arduous duties through the cold snows of winter, he is to be thrown carelessly aside as useless! I never will believe it, never!

We really begin to think that Father is better; his hand begins to look better, and he is in better spirits. Yesterday he took some grimmy lobelia. He asked me to request you to bring down some of your homeopathic medicine, if you come, which the Lord grant. . . .

Please write all further particulars about old Pachy. When you come, we will sit up three nights & three days, & you will tell us all about that darling hoss. How he caprioled around your wigwam & careered before your *wagin* will be fruitful themes of conversation. . . . I want to get a copy of "The Sandpiper."

        Yours affectionately,
        Grans

* * *June 15, 1864* * *

Dear Sister,

As I am in the last stages of mental & bodily exhaustion, I can write but a very short letter. Your kind letter came all safe, for which many thanks. The mosquito bars came today, & Father desired me to tell you that he can pick up the rest of the things here, so you needn't purchase anything more. If there is any more to pay on the mosquito bars, &c., he wishes you to write him how much is required.

Poor Father was quite sick yesterday with a pain in his side, & for a time was in great agony. Lobelia (blessed medicine) eventually relieved him. We are getting along pretty well, except that the grimmy work still hangs by. We have expended about $4000 so far. It looks *dubrious*.

We begin to think that the housekeeper is a dead failure, but I won't bother you with our troubles. We have found out since we commenced business that honest men are very scarce.

The steamer won't commence to run till the 1st of July. Bocky arrived all safe from Boston after a stormy passage of two days. Mother was pleased with her birds. Did yours fly out of the window? . . . . Some of your friends were here the other day: Hoxie by name, from Artichoke Mills.[1] God bless my dear sister, and happiness attend her.

       Affectionately,
       Grans

1. Hoxie by name, from Artichoke Mills: See Foreword, p. xiv. Curzon's Mill was situated on the Artichoke River, a tributary of the Merrimack; hence the designation "Artichoke Mills."

* * *July 18, 1864* * *

Dear Sister,

Your good letter of the 14th came today. I meant to have written to you a long time ago, but have not succeeded, as you may know. The napkins &c. came all safely, & splendid they are, & so are the shirts. You are very good to us. Mr. Weiss seems to be enjoying himself immensely. Isn't he splendid? There never was his like before or since. Mabel[1] is the most lovely little girl in the world. Father keeps about the same. He goes out on the piazza most every day, & seems to enjoy himself pretty well. Mother has been quite unwell but is all right now. . . .

Would to the Lord you could hear Mrs. M.'s poem as read by Mr. Weiss. We had a large party here a few days ago. I could relate many of their charming little adventures, but I am too sleepy. One chamber door was annihilated, so you may imagine what a rampageous crew they were. Everything is going on pretty well with us except that we haven't got boarders enough to pay expenses. Mr. Weiss has been expecting Mr. Thaxter every day for a week past. When are you coming? Why don't you come now & stay all summer? If you can't do better, run away & leave the old man in the lurch. Mrs. Mason is composing a *pome* in honor of the Island rose—that's you, you know.

Father & Mother send loads of love to you. I suppose I have forgotten everything you care to know.

With much love,
Grans

1. Mabel: Weiss's daughter.

* * *October 16, 1864* * *

Dear Sister,

. . . It is rumored that Reverend Beebe is going to purchase the Parsonage & that he will reside at Gosport for the remainder of his life. Thomas Leeghe of Smutty & Mrs. Clark, who were once the bitterest enemies, are now the warmest friends! We got a good letter from Mr. Weiss a short time since. Bocky is going to answer it tonight. . . . Father is about the same, better if anything, & Mother is in good health & spirits, only she worries about her dear child at Newtonville.

Everybody sends loads of love. Bocky has just come in (I am writing in the south parlor). He has got a large goblet of brandy punch. Sarah Lamprey[1] has not yet arrived. Mother says she has got peachy cheeks!!!

Your affectionate
Grans

1. Sarah Lamprey: Born in 1842, the daughter of Uri Lamprey of Hampton, a prominent leader of the Democratic party in New Hampshire. As will be evident in subsequent letters, she had been picked by Leavitt, the lighthouse keeper, as a suitable mate for Bocky.

* * *October 24, 1864* * *

Dear Sister,

Your cheering letter of the 20th came this morning with the photograph enclosed. The photograph is splendid; when Mother beheld it she shrieked so violently with delight that the pollock fishermen off Peter Mathes Rock[1] raised their heads in astonishment, & Bocky came rushing to the rescue, imagining nothing less than that the grim destroyer was at hand. . . . Father seems to be about the same. He still sits out on the piazza when the weather is pleasant. Bocky & I have been at work on our schooner lately, as she was somewhat out of repair. Day before yesterday was very pleasant, & Mother took a row over to White Island with me. . . . That same day Polly escaped from the clutches of Bridget, & flew with rapidity behind the house & over the hills & far away.[2] It was several hours before she was found. Mother was afraid that she would be gobbled up by a hawk, but Bocky assured her that no hawk ever existed that could cope with that vindictive bird.

We have not got over to Mother's yet,[3] but expect to in the course of a week or so. We were surprised the other evening by the arrival of a couple of gents from Boston. They went away yesterday. . . .

Affectionately,
Grans

1. Peter Mathes Rock: A submerged ledge about three miles southwest of White Island.
2. far away: In *Ninety Years* Oscar tells of a similar escape, though his account would make it a different Polly, one given to Mother Laighton by Christie Rymes in 1873. According to Oscar, Poll could swear in three languages. "One day Poll got out doors and flew to Smuttynose. One of the men there, thinking it was a hawk, was about to shoot, when Polly sung out: 'You go to hell!' The man fled."
3. over to Mother's yet: Cedric refers here to the move which he and Oscar would make into winter quarters at their parents' new cottage.

* * *   *   November 30, 1864   *   *

Dear Sister,

It seems about a month since we heard from you, & it is ten days since we heard from the continent. We have been pretty busy lately constructing a breakwater, & have built about a hundred feet of it. It is to extend from the black ledge over to Little Island, a tremendous job, which will last for years. The object is to make a harbor of the upper dock, so a boat will lie there perfectly safe in the severest gales. Oh, my dear Skipper Grans, I fell down & about broke my knee today.

It is the hope of all the family that you survived the Thanksgiving siege. Your mother thought of you all that day, & held up her hands, exclaiming, "The poor dear child, I wish she could have her Thanksgiving with me." We had an elegant dinner of roast duck & delicious apple pie & cream, much better than a hundred courses. . . .

Miss Lamprey has been gone over a week. She is a very amiable young lady and we miss her, especially Mother, who seems quite dull & sick. I wish you could be with us this winter. Father continues about the same. Bocky wishes me to tell you that he is reading "November." I shall be delighted if you write some prose pieces for the *Atlantic*. I am going to subscribe for it for another year. I forget whether I told you that we have moved up. The event happened on the 8th. Too sleepy to write more.

Your aff. Grans

*   *   December 15, 1864   *   *

Dear Gwammy,

. . . Yesterday we were so fortunate as to get the mail, & more fortunate still to get a nice long letter from you. Bocky & I were out in the barn when it came, massacring Taurus the bull, so we had a good time after the job was finished reading your letter & the papers. The indefatigable Mrs. Clark brought the mail out, & brought it over notwithstanding the fierce & chilly wind. Nothing very frightful has happened today. Mother is much better, & to the joy of everybody has been out in the kitchen several times.

Dear Father feels the cold weather a good deal but is so good & patient. This morning Bocky hastily arose from the breakfast table & in an insane manner procured his drawing materials & drew a singular looking diagram. When completed he waved it over his head, & muttering something about "invention, patent, & power," he rushed off to the shop, where he has been all day. I went out in the shop this evening to see what he had made. I discovered nothing but a piece of hard-wood with a large hole bored in it. Bocky gave it the scientific name of *cylinder*. I have reason to suspect that his invention is not a perfect success, for he is hard at work this evening drawing more diagrams, & every now & then he looks up & laughs. And well he may, for Gasping Death is convulsed with merriment out in the kitchen over her spelling lesson, which she is reciting to Lizzy. Such unearthly & dying & grimmy groans I never heard. . . .

Bye the bye, what do you make of the presidential 'lection? I read the account of the suffering & starvation of the Union prisoners in the South. What incarnate demons our Southern brothers must be if all accounts are true. But are they true? . . . Polly is in exuberant spirits, & day after day the monotonous "Pepper box" echoes through the house. It seems monstrous to think that a pepper box should go echoing through the house, but I must trust to your acuteness to rescue my meaning. Gasping Death & Lizzy have gone to bed & Bocky is just going, & I guess I will go too, so good bye till tomorrow evening.

Dec. 16th, evening. This has been overcast & chilly, but the ocean has been comparatively smooth, which is a grateful change from the frothing surges of the past week. Matters within doors are really getting quite prosperous. Mother is much better today & has been up & out in the kitchen nearly all the time. Father seems quite bright this evening, & told me a short time ago that he began to think that the cold weather rather agreed with him than otherwise. He says he feels much stronger—even spoke hopefully of getting about once more.

This morning, as soon as breakfast was over, Bocky seized his beloved diagram & rushed for the shop. But he appeared again at noon in a state of mind bordering on disgust. All his pieces which he worked so carefully yesterday turn out to be useless; they are split into a thousand pieces. "Such is life," & Bocky is still sighing for a "power." At the present time he is restlessly walking the floor & drinking coffee. . . .

Mother gave a long message for you, the substance of which was that you were killing yourself with work. Mother herself is worrying very much about the draft. I really believe the constant worry caused her illness. . . .

Affectionately,
Cedy

* * *December 28, 1864* * *

Dear Gwammy,

The inhabitants of Appledore are all attacked by grimmy colds in their heads. Diphtheria will soon succeed, I suppose, & then, "Come, good grimmy Death! Your victims are ready." We have had pretty severe weather. Last Thursday night was very cold; the wind blew with violence from the northwest, & the windows in the kitchen were deeply covered with white frost. About midnight the cold became so great that Father & Mother were forced to leave their room, which is the N.W. corner room, you know. They retreated to the dining room, where a brisk coal fire was burning, making the room genial. Father sat comfortably in his chair; Mother improvised a temporary bed out of a small cot bedstead. It was indeed temporary, for poor Mother had scarcely cast her wearied frame upon it before the frail & unsubstantial fabric gave way, & utter ruin was the consequence. Alas for the insignificant works of man. There is nothing that human art has produced that will withstand the rolling tide of circumstances. Poor Mother passed a sleepless night upon the floor, but with her usual unselfishness forbore to arouse her somnolent household. When morning came, the story was told to her awestruck sons, who with melancholy faces & uplifted hands gave such sympathy as their feeble brains were capable of. After the heart-rending recital the aforesaid sons dashed the tears away from their weak, gray eyes, & seizing their milk-pails, slowly departed for the barn. The day was enlivened by the arrival of the mail, & in it were two nice long journal letters from you. . . .

I wonder how my dear Gwammy enjoyed Christmas. We had a pretty gay Xmas dinner, consisting of turkey, ducks, & pudding. Bocky & I got drunk in the evening & we confabulated till a late hour on topics of great interest, which, however, are hazy in my mind today. Grimmy received an invitation from her relatives at Smuttynose, but she did not go over.

What is your opinion of the Great Rebellion? Is the end near, or is there to be another term of bloodshed? Our President has called for three hundred thousand more men. Men do not seem to volunteer now; that's a bad sign.

Mother, I think, has quite recovered from her illness, & Father certainly grows no worse. Bocky has been busy lately making a large windmill to pump water from the well into the tank. We all send wishes for your happiness New Year's day. . . .

                        Affectionately,
                        Grans

* * *January 1, 1865* * *

Dear Gwammy,

I have just placed your last letter (Dec. 20th) on the upper part of my desk so I can gaze with feelings of intense delight upon that beautiful stork you "drawed." Anybody can see it was the work of a moment, & yet its graceful proportions, gleaming eye, & elongated beak attest to the skill & genius of the artist. Allow me to thank you, dear Gwammy, in the name of the whole family, for drawing that "incongruous" bird. . . .

Lizzie Hoyt went home about a week ago, & yesterday Julia Somebody, who was here two summers ago, came. She is quiet & seems to be quite a good sort of a girl. Being a daughter of the Emerald Isle, she was warmly welcomed by Grim Death. . . .

Mother has been reading *John Halifax* to Father, & they seem quite interested in it. I got some of your old letters this forenoon & reread them & was much edified thereby. I noted as a singular fact that every letter ended in this way: "From your *sleepy* sister," or words to that effect. . . .

                        Tenderly thine,
                        Grans

* * *January 4, 1865* * *

Dear Gwammy,

Bocky started for Portsmouth yesterday afternoon about three o'clock. The ocean was glassy; there was not a breath of wind excepting two or three little catspaws which looked like schools of herring. Bocky's boat rolled sluggishly on the tops of the long swells but didn't go ahead a bit. I took a look from the top of the house at sunset, & there I saw the poor boy wholly becalmed about two miles off; but way off, beyond Square Rock,[1] the water was rippling before a gallant southwest breeze, which spread rapidly over all the ocean. Bocky must have hailed it with great delight. . . .

Jan. 6th. Another pleasant day, dear Gwammy. The snowdrifts have settled quite perceptibly today, & in many places the earth is visible. The wind blows gently from the southwest. This afternoon I took a row over to White Island, & gave Mr. Leavitt the book (*Thalatta*) that Miss Jackson sent him. He seemed very much pleased with it, & I went up to the house, & Mrs. L. gave me a small package for Mother from Miss Lamprey. It began to rain pretty soon after I got there, so I didn't stop long. On the way home I saw lots of gulls & meowls, but they were very wary, & took good care to keep out of gunshot. When I got home, I gave the package to Mother, & with trembling hands she opened it, & there was a most splendid photograph album, a real gorgeous one, capable of holding fifty photographs. . . . Mother was very much pleased with it. . . .

From yr. aff. Grans

1. Square Rock: A bare rock just southwest of Lunging Island.

* * * *January 25, 1865* * *

Dear Gwammy,

This ink has been frozen & thawed so many times that it begins to be rather faint. This morning I put the ink-bottle on the stove & forgot it till the ink began to boil & bubble out of the mouth.

After leaving you last Sunday evening, Miss Swett & I had a delightful ride to Belmont, & then Mr. Simonds very kindly took me to Boston & we had a most gorgeous sleigh ride. The horse went like the wind & the runners of the sleigh struck fire. Monday morning I took the seven o'clock train & arrived in Portsmouth at ten o'clock in the midst of a heavy S.E. snowstorm. I rushed down to the wharf & found Johnson was about starting for the islands; so I launched my boat & tied it to Johnson's vessel & got all my things aboard. Meanwhile the storm increased & the snow came down furiously, so Johnson gave up the idea of going out that day. Saw John Cook in Portsmouth, who made some touching inquiries for Mr. Thaxter & family. Heard various rumors that Father was very sick & that our schooner was gone, &c., which of course made me more anxious to get out.

Tuesday (yesterday) the wind blew furiously from the N.W. until three o'clock, & then it died away, & Johnson made sail & we shot away from Ports. in fine style. A few minutes & we were outside of Whale's Back,[1] where the ocean flashed "with cheer & sparkle & delight," though in a way suggestive of Arctic regions, for it was pretty chilly. In the distance the islands seemed lifted from the sea, & were apparently floating in the air, & the line of coast was apparently twisting itself about like a snake. We had a very quick passage, reaching the islands in little more than an hour. We passed close to the North Head, & by Broad Cove, & anchored under the lea of the southeastern rocks, & I rowed into Broad Cove, where I found Bocky & the boy waiting for me. Bocky said everything was right, so my mind was relieved & we went up to the house & Father & Mother seemed pleased to see me. Father seemed to be about the same; I don't see that he is any worse, anyway.

The first thing I did was to tell Mother about you & the Jenks family, at which she was greatly astonished, & says she does not know what to think of your going into a house & telling the inmates it smells like rotten cabbage. I told Mother that the Jenks had sworn deadly revenge & that they had got a cannon mounted in the garret window; so after you are killed you must write to us immediately; you can through a medium, you know. . . .

> With much love,
> Yr. aff.
> Grans

. . . In the *Young Folks* I see you are pictured.[2] Can it be?

1. Whale's Back: More commonly called Whaleback today, this is a ledge with a lighthouse at the mouth of the Piscataqua River.
2. I see you are pictured: The first printing of "The Sandpiper," in *Our Young Folks* for February 1865, was accompanied by a rather theatrical sketch of a woman gathering driftwood under the threat of thickening clouds and surging seas.

* * *January 27, 1865* * *

Merciful Heavins, dear Gwammy, a terrible event has occurred just this moment. Bocky & I, sitting in this old south parlor gazing moodily out of the window at the monotonous snowbanks & the heaving ocean, beheld a boat tossing upon the waves. On the middle seat sat a man rowing, & in the stern—no, no—I never shall be able to tell you, it is too terrible, it cannot be true, & yet there is Leavitt just rowing away after landing Miss—no, no, rather let me rush up to Mother's cottage home & ascertain with certainty if it is she. Could a woman do that? My brain is on fire; the ink with which I am writing looks red, & ever and anon a weird shriek involuntarily breaks from my pallid lips, & poor Bocky is groaning like one bereft of reason. Good heavins! Am I dreaming? It surely, surely cannot be; I rush to the window. Everything is quiet, the cottage looks as usual, the declining sun sends its bright rays slantwise across the windows, & the large panes gleam & seem to say, "We could a tale unfold." Heavings! They are coming. Farewell!!! They knock, they enter, 'tis Miss Lamp——!

Since I spasmodically penned the last words of the above, an hour has gone by, the western sky is illumined by a cold but gorgeous sunset, the western wave is aflame, & the white sails of distant coasters flash, recede, & vanish as did my poor wits when she entered this room. Oh for a pitying sister to sympathize with in this terrible affliction. Do you, O kind Gwammy, love your brothers? I listen for an answer. The cold west wind sighs through the crevices of the windows, the waves beat dolorously upon the shore, but there is no comforting voice. Alas! alas! We are victims and alone. She asked us if we did not see her when she landed, & we said No! We lied with the utmost coolness. To what desperate straits can men be driven? But what will the austere head of this miserable family say? Methinks that upon his brow a portentous frown is even now gathering, & pretty soon the storm will burst. Is there no escape? Ah yes! The ocean! To leap into its depths would be joy—relief. Shall I? I am sorely tempted. It would be justifiable, I think. Miserable wretch that I am, what am I talking about? Suicide is foolish & cowardly. I will find relief in the flowing bowl. Ha! Ha!! Ha!!! Bring me California wine, Catawba, Champagne. Concoct me a brandy-punch, O Bacchus, & in that exhilarating beverage I will drown the recollections of this fearful event. Alas, what an evening is before us! It is already dusky; a few moments, and we shall be called for, miserable wretches that we are.

In all my misery, I can think joyfully of you, quiet & serene in your distant home. O Gwammy, think of your brothers this evening. But how can you? You know not of their suffering. What have we done to merit this terrible misfortune? Can I ever survive it? I begin to think not. The room begins to whirl about me. Chairs & books & tables seem to be dancing, & above them all is a bottle of brandy that wags its long neck seducingly.

With terrible foreboding of impending gloom, I subscribe myself, hurriedly but affectionately,

Grans

* * *January 28, 1865* * *

Dear Gwammy,

This is a lovely evening, though the day has been chilly & blustering & altogether unlovable. But now the N.W. wind has ceased to howl & the ocean is comparatively calm. The new moon is slowly sinking in the west, & the stars twinkle brilliantly. Even now, though the sun has long since set, a faint rosy hue lingers over the horizon. I seize this moment to write you a short account of the day's adventures while Mother & Miss L——(No! no!) are preparing for a game of whist. O horrid game! We played it last night till my jaws ached from gaping.

Mr. Leavitt was over this afternoon, & he discoursed most eloquently on matrimony to Oscar, saying that if he had to live his life over again, he would marry the day he was twenty-one, & that he was sorry to see a young man who did not take advantage of such a splendid chance. Altogether Leavitt seemed so mad & indignant that Bocky was sensibly affected, & immediately mixed a goblet of brandy & water—hot—for the expounder of matrimony. This mixture was as effective in this case as it is in every other, for Leavitt was almost instantly propitiated, & departed with a countenance beaming with affection.

Did you ever taste mussels fried in crumbs? Anything more delicious was never seen, in my opinion. I wish I could send you some, so Mr. Thaxter & Mr. Weiss could try them. To think that we have lived here twenty-five years in total ignorance of this delectable dish! But hark! I hear footsteps outside; alas! the whist party has arrived; so good night, dear Gwammy.

Jan. 29th. Evening. Last evening I fondly imagined that the horrid northwester was done, but we have had another day of it, & cold & disagreeable it has been. This evening is rather pleasanter; the wind has gone down but will rise by tomorrow, I suppose. We had some mussels, fried in crumbs, for supper this evening, & a splendid supper they made. When do you think you will be able to come to the island? I long to see you, & feel astonished I didn't hug you more while I was in California Street. It seemed then as if I should see you always. I meant to have asked you to sing "Wandering Willie" & forgot it. . . . I am writing in our den, the old south parlor, & Bocky & Miss —— are sitting close by, reading. With this incredible passage I must bid my dear Gwammy good night.

Jan. 30th. Evening. Well, dear Gwammy, this day has been quite mild & pleasant for January. The water has been dripping from the eaves, & the mercury has been above the freezing point. At noon, when the tide had risen sufficiently, we got the little schooner, *Lone Star*,[1] out of the dock with the intention of going to Portsmouth, but while we were pushing the boat through the channel, a big wave came along which carried the stern of the boat onto the rocks, & the rudder was smashed; so we hauled back again to await the next low tide for repairs. . . .

We have not received *Our Young Folks* yet, so Mother has not had the intense satisfaction of gazing upon that beautiful picture which adorns the magazine & the pretty little poem, & gives one such a good idea of you as you are supposed to be, on the bleak sea-beach with the sandpiper.

As Capt. Johnson said when we came out of Ports. in regard to the weather—in regard to the L—— case I say it looks *dubrious*. . . . We are going to have some more whist tonight, & the time draws near for the sacrifice, so farewell for the present, dear Gwammy.

Jan. 31st. Evening. The last day of January, eighteen hundred & sixty-five, is gone the way of all days, & the evening comes with black clouds & sighing winds. This morning while the tide was out, Bocky & I fixed the rudder of the *Lone Star*, & about twelve o'clock, as the wind blew gently from the southwest, we made another attempt to haul out. We were quite successful this time, having gained some experience in the former trial, & Bocky sailed gallantly away with the boy for mate & Miss L——(No! No!) down in the cabin. Sweet Gwammy, I wish you were here tonight, for I am all alone in the south parlor here, which is our den, you know. The island seems doubly desolate when Bocky is gone, & I actually think that some sort of society is necessary to the happiness of poor humanity; but it is pleasant to talk to my sweet Gwammy a little, however. I should have sent this letter today, but Bocky carried in three letters for you, so I thought I would continue a few days longer & send in by one of the Star Island boats.

Last night I felt very sleepy & retired early, leaving Miss —— No! No! & Bocky alone together. The meek appeal of the youth's face as I left the room was quite touching, but being hard-hearted I noticed it not. I soon fell asleep & was lost in dreams, which I will not relate to you though they were exceedingly pleasant. I should judge I had been asleep about an hour when I awoke suddenly & heard a scuffle of some kind going on in the entry, mingled with a smothered laugh. My soul sank within me, & my heart gave a great bound, sending the blood with painful celerity to the very tips of my fingers, for I instantly divined that Bocky was again a sufferer. And alas! I was right, for poor Bocky soon came upstairs looking very much like a martyr, & told me in a broken voice that she had actually slobbered him! Now isn't this terrible? Sweet Gwammy, can you explain it? I trust all young women do not act in that way; if they do, another Deluge would be very appropriate just now. Mother was quite overpowered by the proceedings of Miss —— (No! No!) & she & I had an indignant confab in regard to it this afternoon in Father's hearing, & the dear old gentleman seemed very much amused & actually laughed. It is seldom that he does laugh now, so there is, at least, one good result from the extraordinary conduct of the resident of Hampton.[2] . . .

February 1st. Evening. .˙. . A poetical letter from Mr. Weiss . . . made me laugh till I actually cried, which I didn't think possible in Bocky's absence. I read it to Father & Mother, & none of us have fairly got over the effects of it yet. I was so hoarse from laughing that I had to mix & drink a punch as rapidly as possible. The reason I object to water is "because there have been drowned therein all sinful beasts & men of sin.". . .

Please remember me to my Partner, who was so kind to me when I was up.

Most aff.
Grans

1. *Lone Star*: This little schooner, which formerly belonged to Jansen, had been purchased by the Laightons.

2. the resident of Hampton: Miss Lamp—— married Joseph C. Hardy of Haverhill, Mass., in 1871. Oscar, who lived to within three months of his one-hundredth birthday, remained a bachelor to the end, although he admitted having been in love time and time again.

* * February 4, 1865 * *

My sweetest Gwammy,

 . . . Feb. 5th. . . . Bocky & I are netting a net to catch salt-sea herring with next summer. We work in the south parlor here, & have pretty good times. Bocky keeps calling for Mr. Weiss's letter. He read it just now with great gusto & yelled out the last line . . . in stentorian accents.

Feb. 6th. Sweet Gwammy, the heavens have been lowering & overcast all this day, but there has been very little wind, & the air has been quite mild. Bocky & I worked on the net this forenoon till the dinner bell rang, & then we rushed for the cottage home, where we found Mother sitting at the dinner table filling our plates with the most delicious clam chowder that was ever made. All through dinner we talked of the terrible girl of New Hampshire; & after we got through I took a basket & sallied down on the long point by Babb's Cove. The tide was pretty low, & I saw beautiful mosses waving their delicate foliage in the little pools,—mosses frail & brilliantly pink, & mosses of the wonderful green color; & limpets & whelks & periwinkles. As I tumbled over the seaweed-rocks, peering into the pools & scratching up mussels, I thought of a small woman in California Street who I knew would enjoy such expeditions.

At sunset Jonsen passed by the front of the house in his new vessel. Bocky & I, thinking that he might have the mail, launched a small boat & rowed out to him, but it seems that he took it out of the office & left it in his fish store & then started away without thinking of it, so we were disappointed. But we were somewhat restored to equanimity of mind by a delicious supper of mussels fried in crumbs, which was seasoned by more conversation about the terrible girl from New Hampshire. This evening Bocky is apparently possessed of forty thousand devils. He is now reading aloud in stentorian voice "The Siege of Vicksburg," & is endeavoring to imitate the peculiar delivery of J. S. C. Abbott,[1] who lectured in Portsmouth a short time ago while I was there. He is yelling & laughing so obstreperously that I shall have to stop here; so good night, sweetest Gwammy. Bocky has just exploded in a great yell.

          Tenderly thine,
          Grans

 1. J. S. C. Abbott: On January 10, 1865, J. S. C. Abbott lectured in Portsmouth on "Our War and General Grant." The Portsmouth *Chronicle* of January 12 reported as follows:

> Rev. Mr. Abbott's lecture before the Lyceum, in the storm of Tuesday evening, drew an audience which looked about as usual, but numbered only 638 persons. . . . All such history readers and history makers as Edward Everett and John S. C. Abbott tell us that never did the world see greater generalship or more "successful war" than that for the Union; but the blatant copperheads keep shouting, Nothing has been done, or can be, to save our country, but to knuckle to the rebels and traitors. We shall see. . . .

         * * *February 8, 1865* * *

My Beautiful Gwammy,

 I wonder if it rained in California St. as furiously as it did here last night. James R. Lowell, who says, "How looks Appledore in a storm?"[1] would perhaps have been pleased could he have seen the huge rollers that were tumbling into Broad Cove at the high tide this morning. I watched them for a short time & they were imposing, for the southeast gale of last night was exceedingly heavy. Duck Island was fairly submerged, & the sea was breaking furiously on Cedar Ledge & Anderson's Rock,[2] & at White Island the spray was flying over the top of the lighthouse. . . .

Bocky & I worked out in the shop till dinner time, & this afternoon we have been busy with the net. At supper we were all talking about you, & I said, "Sister is the most beautiful woman I ever saw," & everybody agreed with me, & Bocky said, "If she doesn't ever find it out it will be all right." But I have been & gone & told my lovely Gwammy all about it, & she will say, "What has come over my wretched brother; I believe he is trying to flatter me." Bocky has got a singing mania tonight, & the room is filled with the melody of his voice. He wishes me to ask you to send the words of "Aileen Aroon." Father is as well as usual. . . .

Feb. 10th. Dearest & most beautiful Gwammy, this afternoon we got the mail & your sweet letter of the fourth; but, O lovely Gwammy, it was too short; you don't love your miserable brothers, do you, dear? No, if they were drowned in the salt sea, you wouldn't care. Why don't you write a few expressions of love to me? . . . O my Gwammy, why don't you write a pome about the song sparrows? If you were to live here through the whole of a dreary winter, & then listen to their delicious songs, I know you would be inspired. I propose to write a pome about one little humility & I, which I shall probably publish in the *Atlantic*, whether Mr. Fields[3] acquiesces or not. . . .

Feb. 11th. My own splendiriferous Gwammy, when Bocky & I came out of the house from breakfast this morning, we little thought of seeing our Partner, but the first object that we beheld was our dear comrade of the winter sixty-one. He had got as far as the rocky path by Babb's Cove when we discovered him, and we rushed, shrieking "My Partner," & embraced all round. We were all exceedingly glad to see him, & Mother was overjoyed with the flowers he brought. . . . We have been talking over old times all day, now & then diversifying our conversation by reading aloud Marie Mason's "Vikings of the Atlantic," (& low be it spoken) drinking whiskey, which, however & alas! was not "Maryland whiskey." The pome seemed to puzzle our Partner very much; he couldn't make anything of it; who can? The charade & poetry by Willie Jenks shocked Mother, & she lifted her hands, exclaiming, "Alas, is the L—— romance spreading all over the country?" & we answered, "Yes, from Maine to California. . . ."

. . . I wish I could go up to Boston with my Partner so I could hug my beloved Gwammy. I have been trying to persuade Bocky to, & perhaps he will. . . .

Lovingly,
Grans

1. "How looks Appledore in a storm?": From Lowell's poem "Appledore."
2. Cedar Ledge & Anderson's Rock: Ledges east of Star and White Islands.
3. Mr. Fields: James T. Fields, editor of the *Atlantic*, 1862-70. He and his wife, Annie, became Celia's intimate friends.

* *   March 10, 1865   * *

My own Gwammy,

You are possibly wondering where your brother Bocky is all this time. If you were here this evening you would behold him quietly sitting at his desk with a pen in his hand, which he wields in a way that would remind you of crowbars, stonewalls, derricks, bedsteads, nets, & cider bottles. But alas! my own Gwammy is not here. . . .

I will not tell you how the rain poured down upon this devoted island today, and how the *Lone Star*'s masts wriggled picturesquely in the breeze; neither will I describe to you the encounter I had with three beautiful male sheldrakes—how their lovely plumes sparkled & glistened in the sunlight, & how they dove under the billows & came up again with little suckerfishes in their bills; but I will proceed at once to three facts which occupy the minds & time of the dwellers on this "sea-girt isle" (popular phrase.) The first item is that Mother's canaries have laid (I can imagine your start of surprise as you read this astounding passage), & the second is that the oleander is in bloom, & the third important event is that the dressmaker has arrived & Mother has got seventeen new dresses now making, & when you come she is going to put them all on together, & you & Bocky & Father & I will put on our store clothes, & the canaries will sing & the parrot will screech & the turkey will gobble & Grimmy Death will haul in her main sheet & howl in her own peculiarly musical way, & thus we shall form one of the most gorgeous & interesting tableaux that the world has ever known.

The following weak lines were suggested to me by a small poem which appeared in the February number of the *Young Folks*. I trust you will like them.

>Within the cellar dark & cold,
>One little whiskey bottle & I,
>The whiskey bottle all covered with mould,
>And I a-getting very dry.
>The wild bugs crawl across the floor,
>The wild flies by my ears do fly,
>As I sip whiskey more & more,
>One little whiskey bottle & I.
>
>Above our heads the floor beams are;
>Without we hear a doleful cry;
>Two cats are fiercely pulling fur
>And trying to pull out each other's eye.
>Almost as far as eye can see,
>The close-reefed shadows shift & fly,
>But we are jovial; what care we?—
>One little whiskey bottle & I.

It is needless to observe that this letter is from
Grans

* * *June 26, 1865* * *

Dear Gwammy,

Your kind, doleful, dateless & welcome letter came today, & the things arrived safely last Saturday. Why do you write in such a disconsolate strain, O my Gwammy? When you come down I will cure you. Father seems to be getting along nicely, & Mother is as dear as can be, but she was slightly worried by the tone of your letter. Things at the hotel are coming on pretty well, though rows are diurnal. There are ten people stopping here at present, & there were about twenty at dinner. The flower garden is coming forward beyond my expectations; many of the things are budded; the woodbines, too, are growing very fast.

Our Gosport friends had quite a row over Mr. Beebay[1] the

other day. It seems that Elvin Newton[2] "writ" seventeen letters to the society in Newburyport stating that Beebay was a thief & had stolen the Gosport melodeon & the medicine chest, tools, &c. The seventeenth letter brought seventeen ministers of the Gospel down from N. & they pounced upon Gosport in the most terrific manner. A meeting was called & Newton was obliged to attend. The seventeen letters were read, & then Beebay produced dockyments that annihilated all the proof against him,[3] & Newton (the descendant of Sir Isaac) retired in disgrace. I was over at Gosport the last Sunday & heard a part of Beebay's sermon. He pitched into Newton in the most splendid style; he said that the devil had constructed a telegraph from Hell to the earth, & that Newton was the operator.

The only specially exciting item of news is that a man from Portsmouth who took dinner here today drank twelve bottles of ale.

Everybody sends loads of love to you. . . .

Hurriedly but tenderly thine,
Grans

1. Beebay: The Shoalers habitually pronounced final *e* or *y* like *a*, dragging out the sound; hence Cedric's spelling of Beebe's name. See Celia Thaxter's description of the natives' linguistic habits in *Among the Isles of Shoals*.

2. Elvin Newton: The son of Isaac Newton, Elvin lived in the house known today on Star Island as Cottage B.

3. annihilated all the proof against him: *Seventeen* appears to have been Cedric's favorite number; note the "seventeen new dresses" in the letter of March 10, 1865. Actually the investigating committee consisted of three clergymen. The charges were dismissed as not supported by the evidence. When considering the complaint that Beebe had failed to hold regular religious services on Sunday, the committee asked to see his sermon notes—which he produced, complete with dates. This was apparently the clincher, for according to the committee this was an unexpected request "for which Mr. Beebe could have made no preparation had he desired to do so."

Although the investigators cleared him, they recommended to the Society that his ministry be terminated in six months because of such a strong anti-Beebe faction in the community. Before the end of that period, however, he was said to be so firmly reinstated in the affections of his people that his mission was continued.

APPLEDORE HOUSE,
ISLES OF SHOALS.
O. & C. LAIGHTON, ... Proprietors.

  * * September 8, 1865 * *

Dear Gwammy,

Your welcome letter enclosing the money came safely day before yesterday, & I should have answered it sooner but have been hardly able to sit up for the last three days. What do you make of this heading? It is the result of a small printing press which Christie sent us. What do you think of having a horse on the island? Bocky got one,[1] which was safely landed last Wednesday. Since then the hand-cart has been annihilated, & human necks have been in great danger. Father has been pretty bright lately, & Mother is more beautiful than words can express. Mr. Adams[2] has built another fence, which goes around the east end of the house, making a yard which when filled in & leveled off will be quite pretty. The *hoss* will come into play when we commence the job. There are about a dozen persons stopping at the house. . . . The season is about over, for which the Lord be praised. The steamer stops running tomorrow. . . .

Julian Hawthorne[3] departed for Cape Ann on Sunday—have you heard from him? Though the weather was mild when he started & everything was propitious, yet it would be a satisfaction to *know* that he arrived home safely. Mrs. Dearborn[4] is stopping with Mother for a few days now.

Please give our regards to Mr. Weiss & family.

Everybody sends loads of love to you.

Sincerely,
Grans

---

1. Bocky got one: In *Ninety Years*, Oscar gives a full account of the transporting and the landing of Black Bess. He recalls that the stable owner was later interviewed by a reporter, whose newspaper came out with an article claiming that Oscar, in looking over the horse, had said that the

timbers seemed sound, hoped the rigging wouldn't cost more than the hull, etc.; whereas all he had said was, "Does he bite?"

Another story, in the *Morning Chronicle* of September 11, tells this about the historic event:

> The Shoalers and their guests, at Appledore, saw a novel sight, on a bright morning last week, when Bill Perkins drove the old "Butler mare" round the Island, probably the pioneer enterprise of the sort. The fact is, the Laighton boys, intending to clear the rocks out of their beach basin and to make a better path up over their hill, & execute other improvements, got Perkins to buy them a horse—a veritable mare, and not a horse-marine, though the idea of such an animal at the Shoals is enough to make a horse laugh.
>
> But no matter—Perkins goes to Sherb Somerby and buys the Butler mare—and if "the old whip" isn't a judge of a horse, this was once a Judge's mare, at any rate. And so, in full view of Old Tom and all who lustily shook their sides,—Bill mounts and rides to the summit—a more novel if not grander spectacle than Napoleon on the Alps; then harnesses into a hand-cart and drives about "the lawn"—then hitches on to the boats, and draws them into winter quarters—and performs other feats never attempted before on *that* stage, at all events.
>
> This is the first horse known by the oldest inhabitant to have ever appeared on Sir John Smith's Isles; or rather on the Appledore, for it is said that a horse was cast at Rye, several years ago, and taken to Gosport on hay spread in a gondola; but of his history of success we know nothing. Suffice it to say, there is no doubt, and will be no dispute, but the proprietors of the Appledore House have got the best horse in town; nor will anybody question that the horseman on this occasion did the thing up in his usual good style and skilful horsemanship.

2. Mr. Adams: Oliver Adams of Portsmouth, who is mentioned now and then as helping with building operations, was the father of Oliver and Ella Adams. Both children became close friends of the Laighton brothers. Ella served for many years as housekeeper for the Oceanic Hotel.

3. Julian Hawthorne: The son and biographer of Nathaniel and Sophia Hawthorne, Julian (1846-1934) was also a novelist. In addition he was an accomplished oarsman, and more than once had rowed to and from the Shoals. A note in pencil on the back of the letter says that on this occasion he was rowing in a shell.

4. Mrs. Dearborn: Identified in subsequent letters as Eliza Laighton's dressmaker.

* * *September 14, 1865* * *

Dear Gwammy,

. . . Mother has been busily engaged for a few days past in making pickles. Heaps of small cucumbers & barrels of tomatoes & peppers are already prepared, & this morning when I went up to get my breakfast she had an imposing array of small watermelons, which she was skillfully stuffing with spices, &c. preparatory to putting them in the vinegar. Such is life!

Father has been rather brighter for a week past, but this morning he looked pretty miserable. Did you ever know such weather? It is perfectly beautiful, but so dry that vegetation is brought to a standstill, & there is scarcely a green blade of grass on the island. It seems as though we were never going to have another rain. The new well still holds out, & we get about two barrels a day out of it, which gives us all drinking water. Water for washing we have to get from the south side.

There are about fifteen people here at present. We tried to shut the house up the other day but couldn't succeed, for they kept coming. But as the steamer stops tomorrow, a few more days will finish it. Yesterday the therm. indicated seventy-nine—the hottest day but one of the season.

Bocky is busily engaged with the horse, making carriage roads, digging out the dock, building breakwaters, &c. . . .

                        Aff.,
                        Grans

* * *September 16, 1865* * *

Dear Sister,

This has been a most lovely day. The sun set in a sky brilliant with gorgeous colors, & the water was indescribably lovely. You have seen it & can imagine it at once. There have been lots of mackerel schooling about the island, & the ocean is full of jelly-fishes. They were so thick off by the moorings that Bocky & Mr. Burnet, who were there, *screeched* at the sight. The gulls begin to soar over Blue Beach Point. Early in the morning coots & loons fly swiftly by. . . .

All the *help* have gone except Lizzie & three girls; two of the girls are the most fiendish creatures I ever beheld. I should be *utterly* delighted if I were to find them both corpses tomorrow. . . .

There is nothing new to tell you, except that the weather is charming & that this is the most delightful part of the year at the island, which you, of course, do not know. Were it not for the demons I should be perfectly happy. . . .

Your aff.
Grans

*   *   September 21, 1865   *   *

Dear Gwammy,

We got your pleasant letter yesterday, & were delighted to hear from you that dear little John was better. Mother says tell Sister to come right down, so if you will set a day when it will be most convenient for you to be in Portsmouth, & what train you are going to take, you will find some of us at the depot on your arrival. She also says she wants you to get her a handsome cap, & she don't care if there is a ribbon hitched onto it; & she wants you to be sure to get the tassels, bonnet, & camphor.

. . . Our *hoss* is getting along pretty well. The other day Bocky tried the paces of the animal, & as he was rushing over the ground at a furious rate, the stirrup broke & away he went over the *hosses* head. It was in the swamp, & Bocky picked out a soft place, so it did not kill him fatally dead.

Yesterday morning I took breakfast at the Parker House in Boston, & before sunset I was ashore on the island again—pretty quick dodging, wasn't it? I wished awfully to go to Newtonville & see you, but couldn't spare the time. . . .

Any day you name, the *Lone Star* will be in Portsmouth ready to take you out. O Gwammy dear, it seems too much to ask of you. Father is about the same.

Everybody sends loads of love to you.

Most affectionately,
Grans

* * *October 20, 1865* * *

Dear Gwammy,

. . . When the tide went down we commenced work with the derrick [unloading coal], & while we were busily swinging sacks, who should appear but Henry, Pip's brother, who told us that Captain Lear & Brewster (another of Pip's brothers) had started fishing at daylight & up to that time had not been heard from. As he finished telling us about it, another boat came over containing two hardy Gosportians who told us that the missing boat had been picked up between this island and Duck. They said the boat was full of water when found & that Captain Lear was found in it dead with his head in Brewster's lap, who although senseless managed to survive the dreadful catastrophe; & after a great deal of rubbing, &c., upon getting ashore he was thought to be out of danger. "Such is life" upon the stormy billow. . . .

Oct. 21st. . . . This evening Mother is all dressed up to kill, & we are sitting in the little parlor with a brisk fire which as usual throws bushels of sparks upon the rug. Bocky has just departed, & as he went off he remarked that he was going out to the shop to have a good time. He has been at work all day putting an addition to the shop which is to be a blacksmith shop. Mother says that the girls are behaving very nicely, & that Bridget is very attentive to the back yard, & Katy[1] tries hard to be a good girl. Father is apparently better than at any time while you were here, & today he has been scolding in the most rampageous manner. Mother says you must not forget to tell Christie & Myra what a good time she had there & how kind they all were. . . . With loads of love from your "sea-girt home."

1. Katy: Apparently Katy O'Brien. There was also a Katy Fitz, to whom virtue came more easily.

* * *October 30, 1865* * *

Dear Sister,

No! I mean my beautiful Gwammy, I love you like the very "darvil." Returning last night in the *Lone Star* before a roaring southwester, I got your trunk full of "raving beauties" & the letters. Everything in the trunk was perfectly satisfactory, & the recipients were loud in their shrieks & roars of admiration. Bocky says tell her to get Mother some of those plain caps for the love of heaven, lest she should wear one of the old kind. Mother was very much pleased with the bulbs, & we are going to fix them tomorrow. Bridget was rampageous over her things, & Mother wants you to get her a red hood like Katy's & two pieces of black braid. Bocky shouts every time he uses his cup, & is continually asking somebody to take him away from table, for he says he cannot leave his beautiful coffee cup. Katy has behaved so badly of late that Mother hasn't given her the hood yet.

Nov. 2. Cloudy all day with dashes of rain. This morning we hauled the whale-boat, *Spray,* up. The folks to whom we lent her brought her back about a week ago & gave us nine dollars for the use of her. After dinner I went over to Blue Beach with my gun & shot a shag.[1] The plumage of this bird is of a dirty black color, so I do not think that even you, indefatigable plume skinner (birds' squeams) though you be, could have extorted a plume from it. Poor Father groaned & cried all the forenoon after fish, so we sent Pip over to Star Island, & he came back with five cod. At low water I went down by the slip after mussels for bait, for said I to myself, something must be done; we must have a regular supply of fish. I was very successful & got a water-bucket & a basket full of mussels; & while I was shelling them I suddenly bethought myself that Father might like a few duck-mussels; so I took a basket & went down again. The tide was very low, & I wandered out onto points that I never had explored before. The size & quantity of the duck-mussels was astounding, & in a few minutes I got my basket full & got back to the house just in time to avoid a heavy shower.

When is the sonnet to be published? You must send us the number containing it, won't you? Mother has just been reading "The Sandpiper," & she declares that there never was anything more beautiful. . . .

Nov. 3rd. . . . Bocky, Pip & I worked on the road all the afternoon, & Black Bess hauled the rocks along in the most beautiful & graceful manner. . . . Mother caught Katy in a lie today, & she quickly & delightsomely & dextrously & forcibly applied the knout. I wish I had been near to have heard Katy's shrieks of misery; they would have sunk like music into my brain pan. . . .

Nov. 4th. My sweet Gwammy, the rain is pouring down in torrents this evening, & the wind blows fiercely from the N.E. Mother has been congratulating herself upon her cosy little parlor, for when the storm rages without she is more sensible to the charms of an open fire. This forenoon was quite pleasant, & we nearly finished the road, but about two o'clock the rain commenced, so we had to give up work for the day. Pip shot a wild pigeon today, which he presented to Mother with considerable pomposity. While Mother was out in the kitchen, a large spark flew from the fire with great precision upon the center of the mat. It happened just before supper & there was nobody in the room, but Mother's attention was called to it by the smell just in time to save it, though she declared it was utterly ruined. But at the same time that she said so, she seized some colored yarn & in a few minutes it was mended so the place could not be distinguished. Father has been very quiet today. Bridget has appeared in her new balmoral & is grander than word can express. It waxes late (ten minutes past eight), so I will bid my own Gwammy good night.

Nov. 5th. Well, my darling Gwammy, this has been a blowy sabbath. I wonder if you listened to a sermon from Mr. Weiss today. Bocky & Pip & I harnessed Black Bess to the drag, which we have to haul stones on, & drove round the house for two or three hours after breakfast; & then we got the saddle & devoted the remainder of the forenoon to horseback exercise, & great fun we had. Black Bess was in fine spirits & went like the wind. . . .

Father has been rather worse today, & has been groaning all the time in the most hopeless manner. Mother is making a sack for herself this evening, & Bocky has gone down to the hotel to converse with old Adams. Their subject of conversation last night was Queen Victoria, & Mr. Adams asserts in the most positive manner that she is the cause of his rheumatism. My dearest Gwammy, I must bid you good bye, as this epistle is getting rather lengthy.

Yrs. till death,
Grans

1. shag: The double-crested cormorant.

* * *November 11, 1865* * *

Sweet Gwammy,

I have just been rummaging my desk in search of paper, but Bocky must have been writing to his Beloved (Miss Lamprey), for I cannot find any piece of moderate size, so I take this elephantine sheet which I imagine must be one of your relics. Day before yesterday the *Lone Star* came out before a gallant northwester, with Bocky for captain, Pip for mate, & several of the citizens & citizenesses of Gosport for passengers. The cargo of the *Lone Star* was immense & various. There were ten barrels of corn, ten barrels of oats, several boxes, & numerous bundles; so many things, in fact, that the sun doused his glim behind Po Hill before we got them all stowed away in their respective places. We took a late supper & then we all rushed to the parlor; & your letters, of which there were three, were read to Mother, to her intense gratification & satisfaction. There was also a letter from Julian Hawthorne. . . . You poor Gwammy, what fearful times you are having with your girls, & how strange that every one of them should drink whiskey at such a fearful rate. Alas for poor Humanity! . . .

This has been a most gorgeous afternoon & evening. . . . Bocky & Pip & I worked on the breakwater till about three o'clock, & then Willis Downs came running over the hill & told us that Charles Caswell (Pip's oldest brother) had just been picked up off by Square Rock, having been drowned while coming out from Rye. How he was drowned will never be known, but he was found with one foot hitched under the seat of his wherry & his body overboard. Pretty soon a boat came round the point with half a dozen stalwart rowers who made the water foam round the bows as they dashed up to the landing. The body was in the bow of the boat, & poor Brewster (another of the Caswells who came very near death himself a short time ago) was sitting in the stern with a handkerchief to his eyes, & poor fellow, feeling very badly, of course. Pip leaped aboard without saying a word & the boat sped off for Rye. This makes the sixth death by drowning at the islands this season. Verily the billow deep is more than usually deceitful, & danger ever lurks on its turbulent or glassy surface.

Father continues to be about the same. Mother says that Bridget behaves exceedingly well & that Katy is trying hard to be a good girl. She got the hood for one good day, & now she thinks she looks so pretty in it that she wants to wear it all the time! Mother is taking excellent care of the bulbs, & we all look forward to the hyacinths. I have begun on Mother's garden. . . .

Nov. 12th. . . . This morning Mother with some of my assistance "shifted" Father; a manoeuvre which I will not enlarge upon, but which was accomplished very successfully. Katy has behaved very badly today, & Mother almost begins to think she will have to give her up as a bad job. . . .

Nov. 13th. . . . Bocky & I have been working on the breakwater about all day, & we miss Pip's jubilant assistance exceedingly. After partaking of a delicious supper of cranberries & dip-toast, Bocky & I came in here (the parlor) & pretty soon we heard Father ask Bridget to move his chair. Bridget tried to move it but didn't do it right, when there ensued a scene that baffles all description. Father shrieked at the poor girl so she didn't know where she was, & Bocky, Mother, & I suddenly seeing the ludicrous side of the affair, exploded into shrieks of laughter that soon became a united howl, & soon the cottage room fairly shook in every crack & cranny, & every one of us nearly went into convulsions. We were all so jubilant that Father actually joined in the mirth.

Well, dear Gwammy, as this letter is comfortably long, I guess I will bid you good bye tonight. . . .

* * *November 22, 1865* * *

Sweet bunch of desate,[1]

I have been waiting for a few days to see if Bocky wouldn't be inclined to swing a pen in your direction; but though he has got his desk up here in the parlor, in the N.W. corner, he has not as yet hauled forth his note-paper with serious intent. . . . Ah! those mind parties, how do you survive them? But as you are a mind yourself, I suppose you find pleasure in it. Did you take the immortal Vedder[2] by the flipper?

Affairs at the hotel are being fast broken up, Miss Merrill being the only inmate of that rambling edifice. She has got a few days' work there & a short visit to make Mother, when she will return to her native bricks & mortar. Katy Fitz took up her abode in the cottage home day before yesterday, & Mother has expressed herself as perfectly satisfied with her kitchen arrangements; so, dear Gwammy, we are to be congratulated on that head. . . .

Never did we have a more delightful Indian summer than we have had this year. It lasted eight or nine days & every day the wind blew gently, like summer zephyrs from the S.W., the dreamy haze hung over the land, & the surrounding sails quivered in the "wind mirage." But the storm of yesterday descended like a thunderbolt & drove away all visions of summer.... . .

Alas! dear Desate, good night. Love from all.

    1. desate: In his letter of December 15, 1864, in a section omitted from this collection, Cedric says: "Your dodge in regard to the *Atlantic* & *Our Young Folks* is a cruel piece of *desate*. O how desateful you are. But I shall purchase the juvenile magazine, so you see your miserable plot won't work." The trickery seems to have consisted in her suddenly publishing her poetry in *Our Young Folks* after her Appledore family had subscribed to the *Atlantic*. I have not found any later instances of "desatefulness."
    2. Vedder: Elihu Vedder (1836-1923), American artist who achieved eminence chiefly as a painter of abstract ideas. He lived abroad most of the time after 1865. In 1880 he entertained Celia and Oscar during their visit to Rome.

*   *   *   *November 27, 1865*   *   *

9 o'clock P.M. My most beautiful Gwammy, we have just returned from a trip to Portsmouth. Bocky & I started in the *Lone Star* this morning about ten o'clock with a brisk S.W. breeze. When we got halfway in there, the wind came N.W. & then we had to beat up to New Castle, when the wind failed & we threw over our anchor right by Henry Becker's house. It required but a short time to haul down our foresail & jib & launch the *Curlew* (small boat on deck): & leaving the *Lone Star* to swing with the tide, we betook ourselves heartily to the oars. Rowing up the Piscataqua of a pleasant day is not disagreeable work, at least we didn't find it so, & although the tide was against us we reached the wharf in half an hour from the time of leaving the *Lone Star*.

When we scrambled up over the wharf, we looked round in astonishment, for there wasn't a soul to be seen, & the whole city seemed in a perfect state of repose. We debated with ourselves as to whether we might not have made a mistake in the day, & had almost come to the conclusion that it was Sunday, when we suddenly beheld a man painting a house. It seems that Portsmouth was only indulging in the same nap that was commenced a century ago, & certainly it grew livelier as we approached the great square, where a few wagons were plying about, filled with vegetables & country produce.

Bocky & I finished our business in a little less than an hour, & then we rowed down river at a furious rate, causing the old & matter-of-fact fishermen of New Castle to look at us with astonishment visibly depicted on their weatherbeaten faces. We found the *Lone Star* all right, & in the turning of a glass we were under way again, with the sails full of a gallant N.W. breeze. Out round Fort Point we shot, & following the western shore we passed Little Harbor & Odiorne's Point, & then on by Wallis Sands & then we luffed up by Rye Harbor. There Bocky took the small boat & rowed ashore to get Pip, & I saw him row in to a small bight & hold some conversation with some men who were gathering seaweed, & then he disappeared behind a sand-hill. As he vanished the sun burst through a rift in the clouds, just over the tree-tops, & gleamed warmly & brilliantly upon the sails of the *Lone Star* & upon the water, which was soon flushed with the most gorgeous hues. Purple, green, & yellow blended most beautifully together, & this with the brilliant clouds & the dark woods & hills & the islands in the distance, to the east, made a most beautiful picture. The glow was but transitory, however, for while I was yet gazing at the illumined occident the gloom of night settled upon the scene; objects on the shore became indistinguishable in the darkness, & White Island & Boon Island[1] flashed into life.

Pretty soon I heard voices on the shore, & as I luffed the *Lone Star* & hauled the jib-sheet to windward, I saw Bocky & Pip close at hand, & in a few seconds the *Curlew* was again on deck, the sails were winged out, & we heard the welcome sound of the water as it dashed round the bows of the boat. The *Lone Star* seemed to be endowed with intelligence, for with her bowsprit pointing at the light in Mother's parlor window, she rushed over the briny billows like a sea-gull, & before we were aware of it we found ourselves by the moorings. It was then down foresail & jib, haul in the mainsail, hard down the helm, & away we went up into the wind & onto the moorings. The sails were stowed in a trice; & grabbing the mail & the provender (hind-quarter lamb & tripe) we rowed into the placid upper dock, fastened the boat, & walked up to the house. Mother had a delicious supper ready for us to which we did ample justice, as we had fasted since breakfast. After supper the mail was opened & your good letter of the seventeenth was read to Mother, much to her delight. . . .

Here's a piece of news for you: Miss Merrill is going to stay all winter—at least that is the arrangement now. She is also going to work for us next season as housekeeper. The charming way in which she cleaned the hotel & washed the sheets, blankets, &c. made a great impression on the minds of O. & C. . . . Father seems to be growing weaker very fast, but the dear is very patient & brave. I have thought of my dear Partner very often lately & should have written to him, but I didn't know where he might be. At this season of the year I always think of him, for it was about this time that he came to the island & stayed all winter, & I wish he would do it again. I never saw a person out of our family in whom I could so fully trust. He is a dear Partner & worthy to be as happy as he undoubtedly will be. . . .

Nov. 29th. . . . This forenoon we killed a cow. While we were at dinner Leavitt came over & brought some fresh cods' tongues for Father. Bocky & I saw him after we had eaten our dinner, & he sadly repeated several verses from Scott's "Lady of the Lake," & taking half of the cow's liver that Mother had given him, mournfully departed. About three o'clock Billy Downs,[2] familiarly known as Happy Norton, came over. Though shriveled with the cold, all in rags, & just able to hobble about, the cheerfulness of Happy was unbounded. He greeted us in Gaiety's own language & blithely retailed all the gossip of Gosport for our benefit. This evening we have all been reading. I have just been in to see Father, & he smiled in the sweetest manner imaginable. He doesn't suffer pain but seems to grow weaker every day. His appetite doesn't seem to be so good, either. . . .

Nov. 30th. "How looks Appledore in a storm?" My dear Gwammy, the Atlantic surges are boisterous this evening. The wind has been blowing a gale all day from the N.E., & the gulls have been soaring over Broad Cove enjoying the crash of the billows & the whistling of the blast. . . . Father has been pretty bright today, & this evening he even indulged in a snatch of song. Mother is extremely well & bright now, though she, of course, has manifold troubles & trials & a great deal of care. This morning Katy O'Brien saw a few flakes of snow falling, & she immediately rushed upstairs without saying a word to anybody & took the best hair mattress & all the spare blankets she could find, & put them upon her own bed. Mother reproved her & she seemed very repentant, promising not to do anything wrong again. But in fifteen minutes she told one of the most deliberate whoppers imaginable. Such is life. Mother says Katy Fitz is an exceedingly good & capable girl. . . .

Yours till death,
Grans

1. Boon Island: This forbidding rock with its lighthouse, about eight miles off York, Maine, inspired Celia's poem, "The Watch of Boon Island." More recently, Kenneth Roberts based his novel, *Boon Island*, upon a tragedy which took place there in 1710.

2. Billy Downs: Probably the William Downs designated as a "cripple" in the list of the Gosport Militia (Town Records, *ca.* 1858). This William was born in 1822, a younger brother of John Bragg Downs, who appears elsewhere in these letters.

* * *December 4, 1865* * *

Dear Gwammy,

. . . Bocky has been at work on the chimney all day, & he has got the boiler, which is a splendid great square one, set as neatly as a professional could have done it. Mother is perfectly delighted with it, & she intends to have a baker put in also. Since Miss Merrill & Katy Fitz have come up here, we take our meals in the parlor. I wish you could be with us & have some of the fried fish & chowder that is sometimes served. And I suppose anybody wouldn't object to a scrod now & then. The sage puddings which we have for dessert are enough to make the cats laugh. . . .

Grans

* * *December 17, 1865* * *

Beloved Gwammy,

Bocky thinks to go to Portsmouth the first chance, & as that may be tomorrow, & Bocky does not seem inclined to grasp his pen, I write today so you may have the latest news from Appledore. I am writing this in the workshop. Bocky is here, hard at work on a horse-power[1] which he got in Boston & which was landed here last Friday. Bocky & Miss Merrill & Pip went to Portsmouth last Monday & Bocky & Miss Merrill went to Boston the same day & got back on Thursday. The mail contained your beautifully illumined & sprightly letters, which were much admired by the whole family. Bocky thought the frontispieces were magnificent, & he went so far as to go to his desk & take out his writing materials, but I believe that was all, for he can't stay away from his beloved shop but a few moments at a time. And when I asked him why he didn't answer your letters, he said he didn't have *time*.

The events of the week have not been very startling. The most exciting event was getting the horse-power ashore, for it weighed fifteen hundred pounds, & was pretty hard to handle. We didn't get it ashore the same day that Bocky came out, as it was too late & the tide was down, & the next day the wind blew fiercely from the N.W., & when we came down stairs in the morning the *Lone Star* was bowing to the N.W. surges, & her deck was white with ice. After breakfast we went off & hoisted the foresail & scudded round on the south side of the island. Then we got the shad-boat & got the power into it & pulled round to the upper dock again. When we landed we resembled the common drowned rats of our country. When we got the power up to the shop it was broken in a dozen places, but Bocky thinks it can be fixed again easily enough.

Yesterday Mother & Miss Merrill preserved a barrel of cranberries in the most gorgeous manner. At supper we had a little plateful of jelly apiece, & it was perfectly delicious. Bocky screeched at every mouthful. But what a tremendous Thanksgiving dinner you must have had! We were all perfectly overwhelmed with your account of it. We had plenty of turkey & duck for our feasting, cooked, too, in Mother's happiest style. Father is about the same. This morning he is in excellent spirits, & told Mother when she was fixing him that he thought he was getting well. But it is evident to us all that he is failing fast. He has got so he can lie on the bed again. He tried it yesterday (the first time for months) with evident benefit. And he is lying down this morning. I expect to be called every minute to help him into the chair again.

Enclosed is a letter to our Partner. I shall be much pleased if you put it in the way of reaching him. . . . The package came safely & everybody was delighted with the contents. Mother says the cap was just a grain too large—too big round. Bocky was delighted with his book!

With oceans of love,
Grans

1. horse-power: "A machine worked by a horse, for driving other machinery; a horse motor." (*Webster's New International Dictionary*, 2nd edition).

* * *December 25, 1865* * *

Dear Gwammy,

. . . In the evening [Christmas Eve] we all hung our stockings up, but Bridget & Katy were a little doubtful as to St. Nicholas. This morning I got up at daylight, & coming down stairs I saw Katy rush into Mother's room shrieking, "I wish you a Merry Christmas, 'Miss' Laighton." I went over on the hill. . . . When I got back to the house, I found everybody assembled with a stocking, so I grabbed mine & then we all began to haul forth the contents. Verily St. Nicholas must have made quite a long stay with us last night, for the stockings were crammed. Mother got a picture, a book, apples, clothes pins, & candy; & Bocky got a picture, candy & apples, & a silver napkin ring & a jumping-jack, which we have kept bobbing about all day. Miss Merrill got a writing case, . . . apples, &c. The contents of my stocking was just like Bocky's with the exception of the jack. Father got a lot of candy in his stocking, & Pip got a gold watch & a handkerchief & some writing paper. The watch nearly drove him crazy. The girls got so many gorgeous things that they were nearly mazed.

Evening. . . . Everything is jolly at the island. Father is as well as usual, & Mother is in excellent health & spirits.

With oceans of love,
Your
Grans

* * *January 4, 1866* * *

Sweet Gwammy,

. . . Father has been remarkably well today, & he took your letter & read it aloud to Mother, who did nothing but laugh, for he read it in the funniest way imaginable. Of course he didn't get hardly any of the words right. He asked me when you were coming, & I told him you would come just when he sent for you, & he said, "Wouldn't it be funny if I should go up & get her?" Mother is in good health & spirits too. . . .

Sat., Jan. 6th. Last night, sweet Gwammy, after I had finished writing, Mother concocted a beverage from lemon, sugar, & other ingredients, & we all regaled outselves with a goblet full, & soon we all retired singing a bacchanalian song, the chorus of which was "We won't go home till morning." Just imagine your dear mother as she must have appeared perpetrating this uproarious ditty; & Bocky with an old pair of spectacles across his Grecian nose; & Miss Merrill with unsteady hands vainly trying to keep the fire from tumbling on the carpet; & your humble servant quietly attending to the vessel containing the aforesaid beverage; & you have a picture of the confusion that reigned in our household last evening.

Well, my own, this has been another day of northwester. This morning the glass stood at eight above zero, & the ocean is still steaming at a great rate. At sunrise, it was funny to watch the coasters as they went by in front, with just the tops of their masts & sails above the vapor. Mother & I shifted Father, & then I went out in the shop, where was Bocky screeching with delight, Black Bess in the "power," Pip with distended mouth, & sufficient noise to drive a nervous person into an early grave. Bocky has got the shafting up & the pulleys fixed, & in a few days he will have his machine running by the horse-power, when his joy will be unbounded, I suppose. . . .

Jan. 8th. . . . Pip has been trying to write to his mother today. "He commenced at morn & left off at dewy eve," but the missive is still unfinished. His attitude while writing is sublime. Bocky has been flying about the shop at a great rate, turning iron & wood & making shafts & counter-shafts & "shippers" & other neat little contrivances. He says that his idea of perfect bliss is to be begrimed with iron & brass filings & oil! I saw a sparrow today by the pig-sty. O sparrick, why didn't you fly south?

Jan. 9th. . . . Nothing has happened today, except that John Cook came over. He came into the shop & remarked that it was awful lonesome over at Star. I gave him a glass of grog & a huge piece of meat, & he went on his way rejoicing. After dinner Pip & I dug a mess of clams for Father. Father seems much weaker than he was a month ago. I have to lift his whole weight now. Today Bocky has got his lathe going by the horse-power. Poor Black Bess thinks she is traveling very fast when she doesn't get ahead a mite. "Come & see us, when you get a cha-ance. How's your folks?"

Jan. 10th. . . . Joe Caswell was over this forenoon & told us many fearful stories. He said that a new ship that left Ports. last fall was lost, & that the yawl-boat belonging to it had been picked up by a Newburyport vessel & that four men were found in the yawl, two of whom were dead & the others were devouring them, having been out fourteen days. . . .

All send loads of love.

* * *February 8, 1866* * *

Dear Conjangle,

The thumb with which Bocky swings a pen is swelled so much & so extensively swaddled in rags that he is unable to answer your jovial letters of Jan. twenty-first & thirtieth which arrived by the way of the *Spray* yesterday morning. So you see I grab a pen to give you the news of the island, & tell you how delighted we were with the painting of the little girl with the watering-pot, & the inky old fisherman. . . .

Affairs at the island are in rather a melancholy condition. When I got home I found Father was much worse, & everybody worn out for the want of rest; so you see I was much needed here. One day after I got back Father was so very ill that we thought he would not live till night, but since then he has rallied somewhat, & is now tolerably comfortable. Someone has to sit up every night. Miss Merrill kindly takes every third night, so Mother gets her rest, & we are determined she shall not be disturbed till the last moment, for as you may imagine, she has enough to trouble her in the days. The other morning, as I watched the daylight coming in the cold, gray sky, I thought of you & the midnight hours of last spring, when we used to eat toasted crackers & drink hot coffee.

One of the frailties of our position is that we are all out of liquor—not a drop of rum, gin, whiskey, or brandy—only a little sherry-wine & claret left. We have got a supply in Ports., & there it is likely to remain for some time, I imagine, for the *Lone Star* is frozen up in the upper dock, & isn't fixed yet, either. O Gwammy, what a miserable winter this has been, so far. How glad I shall be when warm weather comes, though I do not think Father will be with us, & in fact I do not think he will live through this month. . . .

Please give my love to all the children & heartiest regards to my brother-in-law. How are your flowers? Miss Merrill has succeeded in killing most of Mother's, with scalding hot water. I have just finished reading *Our Mutual Friend,* which has got a "fatal freshness upon it." Bocky is now reading it & is at the present moment screeching over "Mrs. Wilfer & R.W." Dearest Gwammy, farewell. I'm afraid you have seen Father for the last time, for at this stormy season it is almost impossible to reach you.

With much love,
Grans

* * *February 14, 1866* * *

Dear Gwammy,

It is my turn to sit up tonight, so to while away the first part of the evening I grab my quill. It is now ten o'clock; everybody has gone to bed but Bocky, & he is just going. Father is lying on the bed & seems to be pretty quiet. Last night Bocky sat up & Mother & I had to get up twice during the night. . . . Unless Father's condition changes, I do not think he will live a fortnight; he suffers very much. The wind blows a small hurricane from the south'ard now, & the rain is beating against the window-panes. Do you know what a wind-whistling house this is? There is a regular concert going on outside now. Up in my room the other night I went to sleep to the whistling & dreamed all night of the most delicious music.

Bocky & Pip & I have been at work on the *Lone Star* for a week past, & today we finished her, much to our delight, & tomorrow if the weather is propitious I am going to Portsmouth to get a load of coal & provisions, for we are beginning to fall short of many things. Black Bess had a severe fall the other day & was so badly injured that for some time we despaired of her recovery, but lately she seems much better. Poor Bocky has not been able to work his horse-power lately, as you may imagine; & if it hadn't been for the accident to the horse, I suppose his unlucky thumb would have hindered him. The poor fellow has been confined to the house, almost, for nearly a month with that same thumb; & when Bess was hurt & one of our boats was smashed on the rocks in addition to the other miseries, he was ready to welcome "Grimmy" even with exultation. He hasn't been off of the island since Christmas. Sweet Gwammy, as I draw near the end of this epistle, sleepiness begins to overpower me. I wonder what I can do to keep Morpheus at bay till morning. Well, my own, I must bid you good bye. Everybody sends loads of love, & Mother says the caps are splendid. . . .

* * *April 21, 1866* * *

Sweet Tapir,

Bocky is just about starting for Ports., so I write this to give you the latest news from the island. Father seems to change from good to bad & back again with wonderful rapidity. Yesterday he was so ill that we thought he would hardly live through the night, & this morning he was so bright & well that we took him down to the big house, at his own request, to look at the alterations. He also made a hearty breakfast of eggs & coffee. Your letter which you supposed Bocky was going to bring came Friday. Mother was delighted to hear particulars of the parrot.

With regards to you, Mum, & with a wish that you will excuse this terrific note.

"Shad"

Mother is remarkably well.

* * *April 27, 1866* * *

Dear Sister,

. . . Father has been rather worse today, though he has been quite smart throughout the week. This morning he looked very badly. His legs are very much swollen & are running somewhat worse than they were last fall. To look at Father, a stranger's opinion (this morning) would probably have been that he could not live the day out, & I think now that he will hardly survive the spring. Mother has been quite sick since I wrote last, but is entirely recovered now, & is in excellent spirits. She caught cold somehow. . . . The *nuss* has been "to Portsmouth" this week. She was gone two nights & returned with Bocky in just such a southerly gale as she came out in before. Her sea experiences are sad! She does wonderfully well, & seems perfectly contented & satisfied.

We have commenced operations down at the hotel. Two girls came last Tuesday. We have been at work taking away the old dining room & building a foundation for the new one for a week past, though the lumber has not arrived yet. Sweetest Tapir, when do you intend to write to your distracted family? We have not received but one letter since you departed. Can it be that you were overthrown by the fatigues of your journey? Bocky has just come up from the other house, & desires me to tell you that he is most dead & that the tar from the mastic roofing (no, no!) has stuck to his face to the depth of an inch.

If you should decide to write at any time, any little items in regard to the parrot, your new gowns, & various other matters would be received with great thankfulness.

Everybody sends loads of love. Please remember us to all friends.

Lovingly,
"Shad"

* * *May 6, 1866* * *

Dear Tapir,

. . . Father has been much worse since I wrote, & it seems impossible that the end is far off. He takes nothing now but a little wine & water, & doesn't seem to know anybody. A good many times since you left if you had been within telegraphing distance we probably should have sent for you. However, we are trying to put it off till the last moment. A northwester has been howling about the island for ten days past. But this morning was wonderfully calm & pleasant, & I took the occasion to plant Mother's garden, although it was the holy sabbath.

The great item of excitement at the islands now is the conflagration on Star Island, which occurred last Thursday night about midnight. Four houses were burned[1] —two hotels, the *Atlantic* & Gosport Houses, & two dwelling houses, Nat. Berry's & Aunt Sally's. Aunt Sally was burned quite severely, & they say that all the property she saved was six plates. Wm. Berry, who was living in the Atlantic House, lost all his furniture, bedding, &c. Nat. Berry lost everything. It is really quite a sad affair. They think that someone must have set it afire, & the story goes about that this isn't the last of the fires on the Shoals; so you, perhaps, may soon receive a sample of the ashes of the Appledore House.

Mother says do for Mercy's sake take good care of the parrot. She says she had no idea she should miss her so. The nurse does very well.

Dearest Tapir, I have written this in a great hurry & I am afraid it is neither legible nor lucid. I hope, however, it will prove better than nothing. Don't be surprised if you are sent for sometime this coming week.[2]

All send love to you & all. Mr. Weiss's lovely letter to Mother came today.

Lovingly,
"Shad"

1. Four houses were burned: Despite the devastation, at least three of the buildings were repaired. In 1875 these were incorporated into the new Oceanic Hotel, at present (1972) the Star Island Conference Center. These were the Atlantic House, now the west wing of the Center; the Gosport House; and Aunt Sally's (the latter two making up the present Gosport Annex). What became of Nat. Berry's house and even where it stood are unknown.

2. this coming week: She was indeed sent for, and according to Oscar, "We were all near him when his brave spirit drifted away." He died on May 18, and was buried on the little hill a short distance behind the hotel.

* * May 27, 1866 * *

Dear Sister,

. . . Affairs at the island are going on very well. The new dining room is finished on the outside, & the workmen have commenced the flooring, furring, & finishing on the inside. We have engaged plasterers & a painter! The painter is coming tomorrow, weather permitting, & is going to commence immediately on Mother's house.

You must not worry about Mother, for she seems very bright & happy all the time, though she says she misses *you* very much. Miss Merrill sleeps with her, & through the day she has plenty of occupation in bringing Bridget & Katy into the double quick of culinary operations & tactics. And then Bocky & I are up here a great deal, so altogether we are getting along better than could be expected under the circumstances. We have received the June *Atlantic, Harper,* & *Young Folks.* The last number of "Griffith Gaunt" leaves us in some suspense, for the grimmy "Ryder steals out armed for conquest." Mr. Whittier tells us of "The Dead Ship of Harpswell," & says "O hundred-harbored Maine," which causes me great delight.

Do not forget to mention to Mr. T. the matter of the *whiskey* & *gin,* as our supply grows shorter daily. There seems to be a something in the sea air of this island which causes anything of that description to evaporate with wonderful rapidity.

Mother & Bock join me in sending loads of love to you all. Please remember us particularly to Mr. Thaxter.

With much love,
"Shad"

*   *   May 28, 1866   *   *

Dear Sister,

If the weather is favorable tomorrow, I intend to go to Ports., so I thought I would write this little note to inform you of the safe arrival of the "licker." Origen Caswell brought it out today, but there was no mail, for which we were sorry. We have tried some of the whiskey this evening in the form of a punch, & Mother & Bocky pronounce it excellent. They, of course, must be undoubted judges of the article by this time. I took my portion of the punch without grumbling, though I thought it very small. Mother has been in excellent spirits today, & the way she has generaled Bridget & Katy has been a caution. The dining room progresses rapidly, notwithstanding the deluging rain. This afternoon we had some tremendous showers; the water rushed off of the hill, into the swamp, in cataracts & with thunderous racket. In the midst of the storm four weatherbeaten citizens of Rye made their appearance, wet to the skin, & touchingly inquired for whiskey. Of such stuff are the men of the present generation made. . . .

Lovingly,
"Shad"

* * May [29], 1866 * *

Dear Sister,

How fast time flies! Here it is almost June, & it will not be so very long before we see you again. Today I have been to Portsmouth & back, & got your letter & a package at the express office containing the curtains. Please tell Mr. Thaxter that I should like the cloth very much. I would enclose the money now, but that I shall have to make a call on the bank in P. first. Didn't you make a mistake in the price of the cloth? Thirteen dollars seemed wonderfully cheap.

Mother is getting along all right. I brought out the painter today, but he was so disgracefully tipsy that we had to give him the afternoon to get sober in. However, he will commence painting tomorrow, & after he gets at it, it will not be much of a job, you know.

We were all very much pleased to hear that Mr. Thaxter is coming, & hope you will all be able to leave home real early.

Bushels of love from all.

"Shad"

*   *   *June 7, 1866*   *   *

Dear Sister,

... Everything has arrived safely, & dear Gwammy, you needn't worry about their suiting, for every single thing is perfectly splendid. Mother is crazy over them. And as for cost, we only wonder how you got them so cheap. Mother is perfectly delighted about the pictures that Miss Robbins is going to paint. The paper could not be more satisfactory, & the painter has not painted the woodwork of the parlor yet. The painter, by the way, seems to have considerable taste.

The carpet is down in the dining room & we have put the soapstone in. The reason we didn't have a grate there was that it would interfere with a range on the other side (in kitchen). We are going to have a grate in Mother's room & another soapstone stove in the parlor. The painter is now graining the kitchen & will probably finish today. ...

Why is a lover like the sea-serpent? Because he is a secreter of great sighs (sea creature of great size). Isn't that awful? Everybody send loads of love to all.

      Yours in haste,
      "Shad"

*   *   *June 14, 1866*   *   *

Dear Sister,

I write today to ask you why you cannot come down before the damned steamer[1] begins to run. You may name any day & we will send the *Lone Star* in after you. Bocky & I have been trying to get some young chickens—about big enough to leave the hen. We have built a large coop, & have got twenty-one so far. We want about 300. Do you or Mr. T. know of any to be bought for 15cts. (or less) in or about Boston?

I saw Capt. Tucker the other day, & he related that the *Pioneer* would not be ready till the 25th of this month. I shall be thankful if we ever can get enough money together to buy a steamer.

Mother is in good health & spirits. She is moving back into the kitchen today. She is longing for you to come down. . . .

                      Love from all,
                      Shad

1. The damned steamer: The *Pioneer*, the first steamboat to be chartered by the Laightons, was built this year expressly for the Isles of Shoals run, according to Oscar in *Ninety Years*.

                    * * *October 7, 1866* * *

Lovely Gwammy,

This sabbath day has been delightful at the island; one of the many balmy fall days that come with soft southerly breezes, & make coast & ocean, vessels & sea-gulls, coots & loons & gumpheads roll along through the smoky atmosphere in the most charming manner.

Bocky, Amos, Pip, & I improved the day & weather by going out on a mackerel trip, by Cedar Ledge. Out there, there were numerous vessels of every conceivable shape & rig, all *hove to* with their jibs down & bait-boxes lashed to the main rigging, out of which the crews were heaving the bait in the *wildest* manner imaginable. Pretty soon we were doing the same thing, & in a few minutes we began to catch the mackerel. It was quite exciting, for the fish were thrown into the boat in the wildest way, & the gulls shrieked overhead, & the mackerelmen hoarsely screeched in the distance, the mackerel fiercely flapped their tails, & the canvas of the entire fleet was slatting in the breeze. But ah! weren't the mackerel delicious at dinner, as broiled by the coy Bridget & served with attendant potatoes, &c. How I wished my mother & sister could have some of them!

Did we experience such fare at the Kearsarge?[1] No! No!! No!!! Did we eat of broiled mackerel at Centre Harbor? I guess not. Did our mother like to perish for the want of a cup of good coffee? Alas, it is even so. But we can all look back with pride, as in our mind's eye we behold majestic Mt. Washington with his wind-swept summit & his dizzy precipices; & I certainly shall never forget Mother's wild walk from the shed to the Tip Top House. And the picture of our dear mother sitting on the sharp rock despairingly groaning, with her unwearied daughter wildly pressing the brandy bottle to her lips, will never be effaced from my memory. And did she roll from the Tip Top House to the foot of the mountain, even unto the Glen House door? She did indeed. Your letter of the fourth came yesterday, & we were glad to hear of your safe arrival in Newton. How does Mother enjoy it? Does she say anything about coming home yet? Tell her with our dear love & best respects that her flowers are in the most flourishing condition & are sending out shoots & sprouts in the wildest way. Also that the coy Bridget has got a large stone pot of delicious butter expressly for her tooth. Do you see anything of Christie? How is Thaxter? How are the children?

Well, I trust that family cares will not press too heavily on my sweet Gwammy, & that her help will prove efficient & good. As for me, I feel as though our family was fast breaking up. Father, Mother, & Sis gone from me.

With oceans of love for all & a universe for Mother,

"Shad"

1. Kearsarge: There is no doubt that Cedric and Celia took their mother on an autumn trip to the White Mountains, and that Eliza returned with Celia to Newtonville. The reader may decide which of Cedric's allusions to accept at face value.

* * * *November 16, 1866* * *

Dear Gwammy,

We have been having a bitter & grimmy southeast storm with floods of rain today. Sea-gulls & coots have been scudding before the gale, & the *Pilgrim*[1] parted her topping lift & pennant halyards, besides plunging her bowsprit desperately into the frothing surges. (Life is merely an illusion.) About noon the wind veered to the S.W. & the sun came forth in unclouded brilliancy, & with the fair weather came two predatory Gosportians with immense milk-pails & other paraphernalia of the chase. (We mortals are but the veriest worms.) These interesting individuals told us of the current gossip of their lovely city. Among other things they told us how one day last week the inhabitants turned out in great force & attacked a keg which was stored in one of the fish-houses, & which contained, previous to the assault, several gallons of whiskey. They said that the whiskey overpowered many of Gosport's sturdiest sons, & that after a while the ladies formed themselves into a rescuing party & bore them to their respective homes. (Such is life.) With many such pleasant anecdotes did our smiling visitors while away the time, & words of wisdom were still falling from their lips as they departed. Their dory tossed picturesquely on the white-capped waves as it rounded the point of Babb's Cove, but the alert oarsman handled his paddles with such skill that it disappeared in a very few minutes.

Mother is still in Portsmouth, stopping with the Dr.[2] I saw her Wednesday & she appeared to be in excellent spirits. She will probably come home sometime next week. . . . Bocky & I are very busy this fall & expect to be while this weather lasts. We are leveling off the hill where the rocks have been dug out. We use a plow, a scraper, & a harrow, & we are accomplishing our object with wonderful success & celerity. I think it is one of the most promising jobs we have yet undertaken. (A few more years & we shall all be under the sod.) The painting, outside, is about finished, & we have reshingled the wings of the old house. Everybody about here thinks the color of the paint is lovely; I think you will like it. Hauling rocks is an excellent remedy for dyspepsia, for with the aching bones comes a most beautiful appetite.

Nov. 17th. Well, dear Gwammy, this has been a blowy day. The waves have been breaking upon the western shore with great noise & commotion, & the coasters passed by with reefed sails. We have all been busily at work on the hill & have done a tremendous day's work. Tons & tons of rocks we have dug out, which the horse drags down to the breakwater. . . .

Nov. [22nd]. Since writing the above, Mother has returned, much to our satisfaction. She came out day before yesterday with Bocky in the *Pilgrim,* & when I went off with the big boat to take her ashore, I found her stretched out on the deck of the craft in the most discouraging manner. But pretty soon I saw her smile. I said to myself, "Well, she is alive; let us be thankful for so much." And we took her ashore & hauled her up over the rocks & put her before a roaring fire; & though she suffered somewhat with a headache yesterday, she is quite bright today, & sends loads of love to you all.

Well, dear Gwammy, it seems quite natural to be living in the little cottage again. I'm writing in the parlor, & we took supper up here tonight, which is the first meal we have eaten here for some time. Bocky is out in his *haunt,* the "Shop." . . . My dear Gwammy, this letter is enough to strike terror into the heart of the beholder. You will throw it into the fire before you can possibly finish it, I feel convinced. But still I console myself by thinking that news from the Island will be agreeable if it does come in such fearful guise.

> "Her sole companions were the two
> Whose manhood years yet number few."

These lines which conclude my letter were culled from that seductive poem entitled "The Vikings of the Atlantic Isle," & I trust they will remind you that you have two brothers who are extremely anxious to hear from you as soon as possible.

With undying love,
"Shad"

1. the *Pilgrim*: A small schooner recently acquired by the Laightons.
2. the Dr.: Probably Dr. William Laighton, her husband's brother.

* * *January 28, 1867* * *

Sweetest Gwammy,

By my halidom & in good sooth, but your letter of the twenty-third was most opportune. Fair lady of the marble brow, thou art in reality beset by snowdrifts, & the opera progresseth in Boston without the light of thy charming countenance. Thou shouldst get into some corner & peruse Whittier's "Snowbound." O my beautiful Gwammy! You should have seen the billows enorme thundering into Broad Cove on the day of the great storm. Monadnock would have clutched his beard in terror if he had been anywhere around, for the breakers rushed over the bank of Broad Cove & whirled the stone wall from its foundation, & pursued the ruins into the swamp. This has not been done since the Minot Ledge lighthouse storm. . . .

Lemuel Caswell is going to get a mule! He has sent a courier on to Washington (?) to procure one for him. Mother wishes to know if you are coming down in wild March, when the throstle calls. We all think of going down to the hotel the first of April. . . .

Aff.,
"Shad"

* * *February 10, 1867* * *

Dear Gwam,

After ten days of mild & delightful weather, the nor'wester descends upon us & the mercury is rapidly falling. Ever since the warm weather commenced, Bocky & I have been making spars. First we made a big spar out of one of the logs we got from Rye. It is forty-five feet long, & we are going to plant it in the middle of the field that we cleaned up last fall. Next we made a top-mast for it, thirty feet long, the whole for a flagstaff. Then we took the *Lone Star* into the upper dock for repairs, & found that she needed a new mainmast; so we made one—finished it yesterday; & this sabbath we have rested, & rolled tenpins! We rise in the morning without knowing what the day may call forth. Verily the ramifications of this life are wonderful. . . .

Mother's flowers are wonderful to behold. Her calla is budded, & one branch of the Madeira-vine is seven feet long. And then there are hyacinths, fuchias, & geraniums in full bloom. "How thankful we ought to be to think we are spared." Dear Gwammy, I discard my quill pen, for I find I can hardly read the foregoing myself. Have you heard from Partner lately? . . .

"Shad"

*   *   February 18, 1867   *   *

Sweet Gwam,

Of all the magnificent evenings that ever I experienced, this is the most magnificentest. The moon is brilliant & silvery, & the air is mild & summer-like, & the little undulations of the mighty deep shimmer & shine & twinkle most pleasantly, & the white sails gleam & fade as they pass by the island. . . .

This evening we have been talking about the spring purchases, & the prospect is truly discouraging. Two or three hundred yds. of sheeting, acres of toweling & bedding, & vistas of furniture; while the grocery supplies loom up in the distance a perfect mountain of outlay. When we are sticking our Gascon noses through the prison grates, you'll chuck us a hard crust, won't you, dear?

By my halidom & in good sooth, fair lady, but thy devoted slave hath no mean skill in a saraband. Shall we join the mazy dance?

While pumping some water the other day, Pip pumped up a frog! It is a chain pump, you know, & how the little creature survived the operation is more than I can understand, but he was apparently unhurt. When through mild April the tadpole calls. I reserve the plumes till you comes, cos they are not worth sending. We are having some mussels to eat; you eats some when you comes. Well, sweet Gwammy, I bids you good bye, with love from all.

Shad

* * June 2, 1867 * *

Sweet Gwammy,

We have received two letters from you since I last wrote, & I should have written before this, but I have been awfully busy, & then I thought Bocky would write. Bocky, poor boy, confines himself to business letters, which are numerous just now. Though this is the sabbath (& a lovely sabbath), we have been hard at work shearing sheep. The flock is reduced to thirty-four, & we have just finished shearing them, having commenced at ten o'clock a.m., & it is now two o'clock p.m. . . .

You should hear the praises your Uncle William bestows upon your last poem. He says you are a remarkable woman, a woman of great genius, & that the idea in your poem is carried out in every line in a wonderful manner. In fact, language failed to express his astonishment . . . & admiration. . . . Mr. Wise, the lighthouse keeper, has been over here several times this spring, & a few days ago he brought over, at Mother's request, about a bushel of small birds that had smashed their brain-pans out on the lighthouse. There were chimney swallows & martins & the most beautiful little flycatchers you ever saw. I wish we could have sent them to you for your pet taxidermist. The steamer commences her regular trips on the fifteenth of this month, so we shall have to run the *Pilgrim* till that time. Though we do not expect many boarders, we think it will be better to have the route established early. . . .

Your affectionate
"Shad"

* * * *September 14, 1867* * *

Dear Gwammy,

"Now comes the winter of our discontent." Today winds up our business for the year unless we take to catching haddock & mottled cod, & we think of it somewhat. Owing to Mother's care, the season has been more prosperous than any of us dared to hope. We have paid all our debts & shall probably have a thousand for you. . . .

About the first of October we are going down to the Nubble[1] for a few days' gunning, with Christie & Lindsey, & should very much like for Mr. Thaxter to join us. I spoke to him about it last spring, & he thought then he might go. Anyway he can come down & see us. We will run in to Ports. in the *Pilgrim* & get him. I will write to him a week before we start.

Bridget, left alone with old Maria, is indulging in some of the most peculiar laughter you ever heard. The cry of the peacock is nothing to it, & sometimes it sounds like the howling & whistling of a N.E. storm. Even the rush of sleet & snow is well imitated. Maria is perfectly silent, &, I should judge, somewhat diskeraged. . . .

Well, dear Gwammy, I have used up all my brain-pan writing these few lines, & I close with loads of love from all & with the vague impression that nobody hates me so much as "Shelay."

       Despondingly thine,
       "Shad"

1. The Nubble: The rocky point of Cape Neddick in York, Maine.

* * *January 5, 1868* * *

Dear Gwammy,

. . . Things at the island are flourishing. Bocky has writ a new poem which appeared in the last Ports. *Journal.* The facility with which the boy heaves his stanzas to the breeze would astonish you. Mother makes numerous inquiries about you all, & I answer as well as I can, but she thinks I am not newsy & is looking forward to the time when you will come down & enliven her with the stories of your winter's adventures. While I have been writing this, Bocky has arrove with the mail & your letter of the third. So you are going to take tea with Mr. Dickens! Well, as you are a chatter-duck, I suppose you will get along well & enjoy it. You writes us a long account of the affair, & omits no word of the conversation!! You will see Bocky the first cha-a-a-nce! It is a cold northwester here today. Mother & Bocky send loads of love. I thinks of you & loves you very much & subscribes myself

Your affectionate brother,
Cedy

* * * *January 11, 1868* * *

Dear Gwammy,

Before me is your letter of the sixth to Bocky, which contains a slight—a very slight—account of the dinner with Mr. Dickens.[1] You know that I am not given to complaining (Lie No. 1; however, to proceed) but I must say that I am distressed,—nay, almost heartbroken—because of the meagreness of your language! To think of your dining with the greatest living reader and writer, and then sending us a letter so full of the names of the eatables as to cause severe vertigo to the peruser. What under *the light of the Heavens* do you suppose we (Oh! peace, good heart) want of Neufchatel cheese! It is too much, too much! Throat of a stickleback, I must have blood! You talk of roast ducks and green peas—*green peas* you said—when we hunger for a word of the great novelist. When we thirst for literary chit-chat, you annihilate us with a bottle of Lachryma Christi. I think I could have borne everything but that accursed Neufchatel cheese! That was the hair on the camel's back. Why so taciturn, Celia? Bethink thee that in this quiet spot the circulation of news is (Oh! that Neufchatel cheese) rather sluggish, and a vivid description of that dinner would have served as an exciting topic of conversation for months! However, we look forward to the time when you will be here; then we shall hear more, for then you will be *forced* to be newsy.

Affairs at the island glide smoothly & pleasantly, though we miss Bocky very much. I suppose you have seen him before this. Oh! (Hash!!) I fully meant to go on and tell you of the sparkling sea, the murmurous tide, and other items of interest; but the memory of that accursed Neufchatel cheese lingers persistently and resentfully in the region of my abdomen. I can write no more! Mother is well and sends Neufcha—Bah! sends cheese—Oh horror! sends *love* to all. She says Aunt Deb[2] would like to come down with you if she can find out when you are coming. Shall I write and tell you how Mr. Wise, of White Island, presented Mother with three beautiful hyacinths, in glasses, and budded? I perceive that the foregoing half gives one the idea that Mr. Wise budded. Well, you must excuse this incoherency. I trust that by the time I write you another letter I shall have forgotten all about the cheese; then I shall be able to write of home matters.

With undying love,
Cedy

1. dinner with Mr. Dickens: Annie Fields, the hostess, recorded in her diary:

> Sunday night dinner Jan. 5 went off brilliantly. Longfellow, Appleton, Mr. & Mrs. Thaxter came to meet "the chief" and ourselves. . . . Mrs. Thaxter's story took strong hold on Dickens's fancy, and he told me afterward that when he awaked in the night he thought of her.

(M. A. DeWolfe Howe, *Memories of a Hostess,* Boston, 1922, pp. 152-54.)

2. Aunt Deb: Deborah Laighton Cheever, Thomas Laighton's sister and the mother of Christie's wife, Myra.

*   *   March 29, 1868   *   *

Dear Gwammy,

This is to thank you for your letter of the 22nd and the paper, both of which came yesterday. Bully for the *Transcript,* though I suppose you'll be so tarnation puss-proud now that you'll disdain to notice common folks. Please don't get to [be] puss-proud, Celia. We send you the Ports. *Chronicle* in which your pome is given entire, with the *Transcript*'s remarks. You are also noticed in the "Local"[1] as an Appledorean and a cousin of the poet Albert Laighton "of this city." . . .

This family has been suffering everything but death for a week past with the annual spring cold. Bocky was taken first and screeched and roared about the house for a day or two and then recovered and retired. Now Mother and I have got it, and we cannot see, hear, or breathe. In which condition life loses somewhat of its cheerful aspect. Mother is continually quoting the "Pocahontas," and "it's enough to kill all the cats" to hear her talk about you and that pome. . . .

Most affectionately,
Cedy

1. the "Local": The *Chronicle* of March 25, in addition to reprinting "The Wreck of the Pocahontas," which the *Atlantic* had published in its April number, and quoting the Boston *Transcript* in full, had this to say in the "Local" column:

> The editor of the Boston Transcript says the poem by Mrs. Thaxter, which we publish this morning, "is one of the best poetical contributions ever made to the Atlantic Monthly." The writer, as is well known, was formerly Miss Laighton, of Appledore, and is a cousin of the poet Albert Laighton of this city.

* *   May 13, 1868   * *

Dear Gwammy,

"O Shannydore, I long to hear you, and I'm bound away on the wild Atlantic." You are the best and loveliest of your sex. Here are numerous letters and other favors that lie unacknowledged. Mother says, "Tell her she is the dearest girl in the world to send me that needle-book. 'Tis just what I wanted and I *am* so pleased." She was also joyful over the seeds. Dearest Gwammy, your letters are refreshing, and I ought to have written before this but have been awful busy and had an idea that Bocky had written. . . .

Rumor says that we are to have another accursed prize-fight at Smutty. Alas that such a disgraceful and beastly exhibition should come off at the islands! Lemmy has just received a big load of lumber and is going to put up a hotel immediately.[1] The *Pioneer* is going to be sold. They have an offer of $5000 for her. She cost, they say, $27,000.

While I have time I will take down from your dear mother's lips the recipe for making beer. First put in your cods' heads—No, no! That isn't it. "Take the roots and boil 'em down together for about an hour. Then strain off, scald in molasses. (Nota bene: The molasses wants to be scalded in the liquor!!!) I put a little ginger and hops in. Then add cold water until the liquor is blood warm; then put in yeast, a half-pint of yeast to a demijohn." Don't throw too much cold water on it, or you won't have luck. . . . Dear Gwammy, please excuse this. Bocky & Mother have done nothing but gabble since I commenced. Mother says she expects Mr. Thaxter and Lony down in June.

Lots of love to all, Gwammy. You are a notable. Yours till death doth us part.

1. put up a hotel immediately: Probably the reconstruction of the Atlantic House, badly damaged in the fire of 1866.

* * May 31, 1868 * *

Dear Gwam,

Here we have the last day of the lingering May,[1] and it is still foggy. (How glazed each weary eye.) What have we done to merit this, and why has it come upon us? However, the fog had one good effect, for it so disgusted the prize fighters that I guess they have given Smutty up. They were most horribly seasick both coming out and going in, and the steamer from Boston got lost in the fog and had to put back. . . .

We have received several letters from people wanting rooms, and we are going to commence to run the *Pilgrim* on the tenth of June. The *Pioneer* is sold[2] to parties in Rockland, Me. She brought forty-five hundred dollars! You will probably see Bocky Wednesday or Thursday, as he is going to Boston soon. Gwammy, you should have been here during this easterly "spell" to help me get driftwood. Bocky and Pip were in Ports. and I got two cords out of Broad Cove, and all the time I was getting it up I sang the "Little Sandpiper and I" to a tune of my own. . . . All send love to you. . . .

1. the lingering May: In Celia Thaxter's poem "Rock Weeds" is the line: "Up from the sweet South comes the lingering May."
2. The *Pioneer* is sold: In *Ninety Years*, Oscar says of the *Pioneer*: "We found the steamboat was doubling our transient business, but she was not a very good sea boat. After a couple of years we decided to build our own boat, to be called 'The Appledore.' The contract for the hull was given to a Portsmouth builder in September, and our cousin Rymes was to put in the

machinery. The steamer was completed and ready to run in June of the following year, and could carry 150 people, making the trip from Portsmouth (ten miles) in about an hour."

* * *Janaury 10, 1869* * *

Dear Gwam,

For the last ten days I have been laid by the heels with Bocky's consumption and have been nigh untew death's door. Expecting every moment to be the next, I have not had sufficient life to answer your letters of which we have had three, which for fatness exceed anything which has yet come under our observation. George Washington's forte was not to let any man of the present day resemble him to any very alarming extent, and your forte is to write fat letters and fat poems and fat tew-hundred-dollar Shoals papers.[1] You would have been amused to have heard your mother and brother talking about you last evening. They came to the conclusion that you are one beauty.

Such weather for winter time surpasseth the human understanding. We haven't had the mercury below freezing for five or six days, not even in the night. The fishermen complain of it. They say their fish don't keep long enough to get them to market. You should see the fish that Carpenter Vultimer Orroarer Inglebritzen[2] (Yes, dear!) brings over to us. He comes about twice a week with a big bushel basket of fish and a big jug for milk. As he is a youth of a tender age, the basket and jug nearly hide him from view as he trudges over the hill. The other day he brought us a halibut!!

Bocky has been at work on the rooms at the cottage lately. He has got one luthern[3] window in, and it looks first rate. Dear Gwam, there is nothing new and I can't write, but this will serve to let you know that we live. Come tew us and don't go from us.

Loads of love from all.

    1. Shoals papers: *Among the Isles of Shoals* by Celia Thaxter first appeared as four essays in the *Atlantic* (August 1869 and January, February, and May, 1870). In 1873 they were combined in a single volume, published by James R. Osgood.

    2. Inglebritzen: A fisherman named Ingebretson, recently from Norway, was renting a cottage on the southern shore of Appledore, opposite Malaga Island. Speaking of his name, in *Among the Isles of Shoals,* Celia says: "Now, to expect any Shoaler would trouble himself to utter such a name as that was beyond all reason. At once they called him 'Carpenter,' apropros of nothing at all, for he never had been a carpenter. But the name was the first that occurred to them, and sufficiently easy of utterance. It was 'Carpenter,' and 'Mis Carpenter,' and 'them Carpenter children,' and the name still clings to fine old Ingebertsen and his family." Celia, like Cedric, had her own variant spelling.

    One of the boys was named Waldemar; it was probably he who brought the fish.

    3. luthern: A dormer window (*Webster's New International Dictionary,* 2nd edition).

* * *January 25, 1869* * *

Dear Gwammy,

I got back yesterday and hasten to write you these few lines, with my pen behind my ear, which leave me very sick, and hope they will find you enjoying the same blessing. There! I guess that's lucid. Your mother and brother were raving because you did not come down with me. Bocky is going to Boston pretty soon, so you can come with him. . . . Your brother Oscar is going crazy to hear the Shoals papers, so come tew us & read them tew him & don't go from us. . . . I dined at the Bigelows', yes dear. Fifteen thousand courses & little colored dishes full of water to wash your fingers to wind up with. It was distressing. I went tew the theatre every night while I was in Boston, & had some fun. . . . Will write again anon.

[From this time on, long intervals between letters are more frequent. Such an extended gap as this one, from Jan. 25 to Oct.

27, usually means that Celia has spent most of the intervening weeks at the Shoals. It was her practice to leave home for long visits whenever she felt less needed in Newtonville than at Appledore. These sojourns inevitably included Karl, as his abnormal development had made him extremely dependent upon his mother.

In the spring of 1869, Levi's physician had prescribed a warmer climate as a remedy for his patient's chest pains. Consequently, in April Levi and the two younger boys left for Florida on an expedition to collect birds and flowers. This was the first of four such trips. It would be hard to dispute their educational value to Roland, who later become a distinguished Professor of Botany at Harvard.]

* * *October 27, 1869* * *

Dear Gwammy,

Yours in pencil written in depots, bejoggled in cars, but still more beauty than words can say, came today. . . . I hope Mr. Thaxter will not come, for there is no comfort to be taken in this house at present. Everything is topsy-turvy; Chaos reigns. The parlors are full of hay, the fields are full of timber, the carpets are up, the beds are down, the dust is a foot thick, and there is no place where a person can spend a quiet minute and look upon anything like neatness and order.

This chaos is the consequence of the alterations we are making. We are building a new barn, and we are going to tear down the pastry-room and put up a new one. We are also going to enlarge the dining room, build a big chimney, put up a steam boiler, build fresh water and salt cisterns, and run pipes all over the house. Then we are tearing out all the sinks and spouts in the rooms, and the plastering has got to be patched and the rooms painted, walls and all. Then we are going to tear down the old barn and the old wood-house and all the old buildings at the back of the house, and pick out all the rocks so as to make a level green. We are draining and raising the swamp by the pig-pen, and we have got to put a thousand cartloads of rocks around the barn. And if I kept on I could fill another page in the same way, but this will give you an idea of the goings on. You'll hardly know the place next summer.

Well, dear Gwammy, here I am at the end with just room enough for everybody's love.

Most aff.,
Cedy

* * September 22, 1870 * *

Dear Sister,

... When are you coming down? Mother thought it was too much of an undertaking for her to come up. Bocky and I are waiting impatiently for the arrival of the rest of the lumber.[1] We are afraid that the cold weather will nip our fond hopes in the bud. And as the frame is to come, we are almost at a standstill.

On the whole we are getting along pretty well. We are putting ventilators into the middle house and are going to skim-coat and paint it. By the first of July we shall be six thousand dollars in debt, but hope to get it back again through the summer. We have got to hire money. How is your money? If you have got much not invested, we will pay you as much as you can get anywhere. Christie with his usual kindness offers to lend us six thousand anytime, but we hate to bother him. He thinks we are doing just right, and would be losing time if we put off building any longer. You have no idea how kind he is to us. He has given us three hundred dollars' worth of iron for the house, and sent us two suits of rubber clothes which must have cost thirty dollars, and any quantity of fruit, &c. It does seem as though we never could repay him. When we do get ahead again, we are going to send him a check for a million dollars. And it isn't in money alone that he helps us, for he talks so encouragingly when he is down here that it is enough to do anybody good. ... With much love,

Most sincerely,
Cedy

1. lumber: The lumber was for the construction of the south wing of the hotel, designed to balance the north wing, opened in 1862. The sketch on p.155 shows the Appledore House after all the main units had been completed.

* *   October 6, 1870   * *

Dear Sister,

Your two letters together with the box came safely yesterday, and Mother is perfectly delighted with everything you got. She thinks the point applejack is perfectly splendid, and the cable chain is more gorgeous than words can express. She thanks you nine hundred and ninety-nine times for your goodness in striving to pick out the best things for her. In the mail also came a note from Uncle Sam with a check to the amount of twelve hundred, for which we have sent him our note, and hereby send you a bushel of thanks for lending us the loan of the money. We will pay you seven per cent for this from date, and also the same for the other thousand from first of January. . . .

The new house goes on slowly; all the lumber has arrived and they commenced to frame last Monday. We are in fear and trembling lest they will not get it plastered this fall, but we manage to eat our rations nevertheless. . . .

All send loads of love to you and all. Mother says you can keep the money, as she may want something more. She *does* want you to come down.

With much love,
Cedric Laighton

* *   November 12, 1870   * *

Dear Sister,

. . . The bear[1] kergnawed his way through the boarded window of the pastry room cellar, entirely demolishing a window sash on his way, and eat up a birril of lard and half a birril of pork, and frightened your mother nearly out of her seven senses. She arose from her bed in terror and screeched to Lucy,[2] so that she might hear a human voice, but that damsel slumbered serenely through everything. Mother thinks an earthquake would not suffice to arouse her. Tonight a hunter is on the track of the bear. Pip is the hunter, and he carries a breech-loading pistol. Tomorrow at seven o'clock precisely that bear's vitals will be toasting over the fire. . . .

With much love,
Cedy

1. The bear: According to Oscar in *Ninety Years*, a bear cub was presented to Christopher Rymes, who in turn brought it to Appledore. The Laightons made a pet of it throughout the summer season. In the fall the bear disappeared completely, only to turn up in the spring, emaciated, hungry, and menacingly big. He raided the lard and pork barrels, and had to be destroyed. Since we know that the raid actually occurred in November, it would appear that the bear was so famished he *thought* it must be spring.

2. Lucy: Describing another incident involving Lucy about this time, Oscar identifies her as "a girl Mother had taken . . . then about fifteen years of age." The words "had taken" suggest that she may have been a state ward. Her maiden name is unknown, but eventually she married Ed (Pip) Caswell.

* * *November 23, 1970* * *

Dear Sister,

. . . The bear is dead, but the night before we killed him he tore out a whole window, so that we had to put in two sashes, upper and lower. We thought that was a little too much for flesh and blood to bear. I can't bear to write about that bear any more; it won't bear talking about (goak).

Aunt Car'line[1] has returned—I knew she would—and she has brought with her a mouth the like of which was never before seen. When she lifted up her hands and spoke of poor Jim,[2] her expression was so comical that Mother couldn't help screeching and laughing, though she felt bad enough to cry all the time. Aunt Car'line is deafer than ever, and when we speak to her we have to scream so loud that we get exhausted with a single sentence. Mother told her the other night that she was purse proud, and says she, "Whitey brown?" Mother repeated it so that the smoky rafters rang, and Aunt Car'line said, "Ploughed ground?" Whereupon Mother heaved a heavy sigh and relapsed into silence. And thus we while away our hours. . . .

    1. Aunt Car'line: One of the servants, surname unknown. The following October 30, Cedric reported that she wanted desperately "to get on the county farm again, up in Brentwood."
    2. Jim: James A. Randall, 33, an employee and close friend of the Laighton brothers, was drowned off Appledore when his boat was swamped in a northwest blow. Oscar speaks fondly of him in *Ninety Years*.

*   *   *February 27, 1871*   *   *

Dear Gwammy,

    . . . We all liked your poem of the "White Owl," though I must say you have written better. For instance, the "Sandpiper" is far ahead of any *Young Folks* poem. Why don't you write another like the "Sandpiper"? But the "White Owl" picture is tremendous with the rocks and snowbirds and White Island in the distance. . . .

    Lucy and Aunt Car'line have been fighting like the devil. The cause of the quarrel is a question as to whether the fair Lucy possessed a skin as clear as Beassy, the scrub girl. Car'line thought not, which led to a tremendous uproar. Finally Mother was called in as umpire. Her remark, that Beassy had the coarsest and most fearful skin she ever beheld, settled the disagreement to the satisfaction of all parties.

    I have been sick for the last four or five days with the mumps! Why should I have the mumps, dear? . . . To think that March is here. Mother, quoting Tennyson the other day, said, "When through wild March the *throttle* calls." Thus we while away our hours.

    Will write again soon. With much love,

Cedy

* * *   *March 3, 1871*   * *

Dear Sister,

. . . Elvin and Origen have been having a squabble in Portsmouth.¹ Elvin floored Origen and kicked him tew a poultice. Origen got the law ontew Elvin and took him up to the police court and broke him. Elvin walked out of the police court intew the arms of Sheriff Morse, who held a writ for assault with damages. Origen laughed nearly intew a cataleptic fit tew see Elvin after a thousand dollar bondman. Elvin swore his life agin Origen, and Origen swore *his* life agin Elvin, and then they both returned to the bosoms of their families. . . .

The Ports. *Journal* compliments your "Great White Owl." Says it is the gem of the number, and that the islands suggest much of your delicious poetry.

Well, good night, you dear.

With much love,
Cedy

1. squabble in Portsmouth: The Portsmouth *Chronicle* carried this report on Feb. 27, 1871:

> Elvin Newton, for assaulting Origen Caswell, was mulcted in $18.04, fine and costs, in the Police Court, Saturday; and on leaving the court he was arrested by Dept. Sheriff Morse on a civil suit for damages to Mr. Caswell, and put under bonds in $1000 to answer the complaint. The assault is said to have been violent and unprovoked.

* *   *March 10, 1871*   * *

Dear Sister:

. . . Did you ever know such lovely weather in March before? The birds are singing here at the island in the most encouraging manner, and crows are flying over in big flocks. Your great white owl is still here. I should think it was most too summery for his constitution. We are improving the pleasant weather by working like horses. We are painting a lot of fifty-one settees, which we bought second hand of the city of Charlestown. . . .

Ame and Pip have gone to Rye to the election, which Ame generally celebrates in such a way as to necessitate his being carried home on a shutter before the business of the day is half through with. When he went off he bid Mary[1] a tender farewell after this fashion: "Good bye, Mary; if we don't meet again here we shall in hell." Mary was slightly discouraged at the prospect. . . .

With much love,
Cedy

1. Amos Jenness was married to the former Mary Jane Locke of Seabrook, N.H. Apparently both were employed by the Laightons at this time. See the letter of March 30.

*   *   March 20, 1871   *   *

Dear Sister,

. . . Inglebritzen just brought over about a hundredweight of fish, mostly haddock. Such splendid fish you never saw; I wish you had half of them. The Inglebritzens got five thousand pounds today. Bocky and Pip and Jud and I tried to name over the several members of the Inglebrit family today and became exhausted before we got half through. We have concluded to name all our tools after them. . . .

Love from all.

Aff.,
Cedy

*   *   March 30, 1871   *   *

Dear Sister,

. . . Amos, after a fearful bat to celebrate the election, came back bringing an empty purse and one of the most tremendous colds that a human being was ever afflicted with. It would have done very well if the aforesaid cold had abided with him, but every member of this family has had it, and Mary is almost dead with it at the present time. . . . Of course Aunt Car'line has got it and has been abed for two days. Once in the pastry-room, here, she had a faint spell and looked whiter than a ghost, so that we were worried about her. We dosed her with champagne till she said she would never do it again; but she retired to her bed and now she won't get up for us, dear. We think she has got over the worst of it, but, you know, she never knows when she is well. Mother has been nursing her in the kindest manner.

Bocky and I have called Pip all the scurrilous Billingsgate names we could think of, because he voted the straight Republican ticket. . . .

We thought, of course, that the quails were either frozen or flown, but last Sunday we started a dozen or more out of the bushes over by the big rock at the S.E. I think they must have burrowed during the winter, as I saw numerous holes where they flew up. And it seems as though they could not have survived that tremendously cold weather unless they were protected in some way. Since I wrote last we have had another slice of winter. "Old Winter hurls a snow-drift at the drooping form of Spring." During the snowstorm the sparrows scurried for the buildings for shelter. One got into the dining room and has been singing ever since most deliciously. Mother sends out seed and water to him. In the morning when we come downstairs his song is so jubilant that we are immediately filled with courage and delight. Notwithstanding the severe weather, the flowers have actually begun to start in your garden. Pansies coming up in every direction, and the honeysuckle has commenced to put forth leaves. Mother's flowers look nicely at present; the fig tree is nearly as large as it was before it was kergnipped, and the calla is the delight of her eyes.

We find the Inglebritzen family a great acquisition. They are polite and agreeable, and are all the time bringing us fish, and take in and bring out the mail for us.

Well, dear Gwammy, I must bid you good bye. All send loads of love to you.

With much love,
Cedy

* * *April 9, 1871* * *

Dear Sister,

. . . Numberless birds stop at the island and give us a song ere they wing their way further northward. This morning I saw hundreds of robins and golden woodpeckers. Also sparrows, crows, wrens, creepers, and lots of birds that I never saw at the island before. Yesterday a little gray creeper flew onto my arm and crept up onto my shoulder. There he sat for a few minutes and looked inquiringly into my face, and then departed in search of grub in a way that expressed perfect content. . . . The erythusaiasamalcuphia has burst forth into bud and blossom. It has sprung from ambush and is trying to storm the world. The blossoms are purplish pink in color and are trumpet shaped. Inglebritzen is farming after the manner of the New York market gardeners. He has dug up and improved more land than we imagined there was over there, and he has got a hot-bed. But you will be down soon, I hope, to see all this. Mother is longing for the thirty days to go by, so don't disappoint her, dear.

Everybody sends love.
Cedy

* * *April 20, 1871* * *

Dear Sister,

. . . You have no idea how stupendous some of our jobs are. Bocky works like an ox, and Mother and I are at him all the time to reserve his energies for the summer. The drainage and the filling in in front of the new house are jobs for a railroad corporation. Mother has been very busy lately on the carpets. With Lucy and Mary to help, she has made thirty carpets for chambers, and I have got them nearly all down. We have got a new carpet for the ladies' parlor of a kind of brownish color, cost $1.25 per yard. We are going to repaper, paint, and furnish the parlor; what color paint do you advise, also what do you advise as to paper and furniture and window shades? . . .

"In May" is perfectly splendid. I cannot tell you how much we admire it. Bocky sat reading it over and over with keen enjoyment, and kept saying, "There is no mistake about that, I tell you that is good."

Pip has been sick for a day or two past, and Mother has been trying to get him to take some pills. It is most amusing that he cannot swallow a pill. He tries them with water, but the pills resolutely refuse to go down his throat. He tries them with rum with the same result. And even with cranberry sauce, the pills as if endowed with life separated themselves and utterly refused to be swallowed. . . .

> Most aff.,
> Cedy

*   *   *April 29, 1871*   *   *

Dear Sister,

. . . Your room looks so beauty that you would screech with delight if you could see it, and I have put an extra mattress *ontew* it. I have put the house to rights from garret to cellar except the parlor, which is to have a new carpet. As to the garden, it is dug and manured thoroughly, and I will see that it is planted according to the approved rules of landscape gardening. Don't spend any more of your pome money for seeds; I will fix everything as well as though you were here.

Aunt Caroline is some at cheering up the weary and desponding heart. Here is our conversation at breakfast the other morning: Bocky—"This is a lovely morning." Aunt C.—"Cold east wind." Cedy—"We shall have to make a glass house for you." Aunt C.—"I don't know which way to turn; sometimes I think I'll drown myself. I tried once and they stopped me." Cedy—"Wait till mackerel come, and you will work in first rate for throw bait." Aunt C.—"Fools to stop me, warn't they?" Mother—"Now do for the Lord's sake keep still and don't have anything to say to her." Aunt C.—"Yes, right down where Jim was *drownded*." Thus we while away our hours.

Bocky has been fairly sick for a day or two with overwork. When night came he used to look about eighty years old. Mother and I took occasion to advance some forcible reasoning against his proceedings, and he sees he is a little *fulish* himself. Therefore he has been holding off, merely directing the work, for a day or two past, and has nearly regained his old buoyancy.

> Most aff.,
> Cedy

* * *May 8, 1871* * *

Dear Sister,

. . . We are tremendously busy. The passageway through Babb's Cove bank was completed today, and Bocky still lives. The derrick with which they were hoisting in the heavy stones broke down twice, and Bocky narrowly missed being smashed by it. The passageway is over three feet wide and between four and five feet deep and seventy feet long, so you can judge what a job it must have been. The rocks with which it is covered are immense.

We like the photograph of John very much. It seems a queer idea to us for him to be on a farm.[1] . . . Hoping this note will find you on your marrow-bones packing your trunks for the island, and with loads of love from all,

Most aff.,
Cedy

1. on a farm: Actually farming was to be John's vocation, though probably such a career was unsuspected in 1871. In 1880 Levi bought an extensive shorefront acreage at Kittery Point, within sight of Appledore, for John to farm and for the family to call home. They named it Champernowne Farm for its seventeenth-century owner, and built a new house, now the home of John's daughter, Miss Rosamond Thaxter.

* * *October 6, 1871* * *

Dear Sister,

I was surprised today to get a letter from you blowing me up for not writing. . . . There is a lingering impression on my mind that I told you of the exquisite fit of Mother's collar. If I *have* heretofore failed in this respect, I am very sorry, and ask a thousand pardons. The collar fits to perfection, and is in fact, as the French have it, "superbe." It fills me with choler to think of it.

Mother is going pretty much all over the States and is going to take me with her as a body-guard. We are examining the papers wildly for railroad accidents, and today have been very successful—a cheerful array of smashups present themselves, if the slightest encouragement is offered. We are going to start from here about the twenty-fifth of the month. . . .

We are still busy with the tank and the shingling. Today a gondola arrived with thirty tons of bricks, and the sand, cement, and lime are coming the first of next week. The masons are coming next Sunday. Mother and I may not get started as early as we anticipate.

The weather is delightful at the islands. The air is soft, and the coastline looks purple in the haze that hangs about it. Your garden is in full bloom. . . .

Most lovingly,
Cedy

*   *   October 11, 1871   *   *

Dear Sister,

What in under the light of the Heavins ails you? You write like a crazy critter, and ask questions and make interrogation points with a repetitive fury that is bewildering to the understanding of the average man. Can't you, *can't* you hold your fulish tongue? Well, why can't ye? And why will you maunder about the collar and the dollar? Well then why can't ye? Why do you thrust the collar in our faces at every sentence? My God of Heavens, the collar fits, the collar fits, the collar fits, the collar fits, the collar fits, the collar fits!!!!!!!!!!!!!!! . . .

The Inglebritzens were astonished to get so much money from you. They don't seem to know what (the collar fits) it's all for. Bocky is first rate, and is hard at work on the tank. The masons came last Sunday and the tank is most done. Your flower garden in its palmiest August days never looked as gorgeous as it does now. The flowers sparkle like gems, and some of the poppies, for color, are wonderful to see. I have saved lots of four o'clock seed—the collar fits, the collar fits. Caroline, after a week of deepest melancholy, begins to take an interest in (the collar fits) life and is making cheese like a common N. A. dairy woman. Lucy was affected to tears by a dream in which she was banished from the island. She was so thankful to wake up and find (the collar fits) it nothing but a dream.

Isn't it fearful about Chicago?[1] We got yesterday's Boston *Post*, which said the city was nearly destroyed and still burning. They must be having terrible times there. . . .

Most aff.,
Cedy

1. Chicago: The Great Fire burned from Sunday, October 8, into Tuesday.

* * *October 24, 1871* * *

Dear Sister,

Inglebritzen has just packed a box of fresh fish for you, which he is going to take in today. He sends them to you with his dear love and best respects and hopes you will find them toothsome. Why sing you of the quails? Oh no, it cannot be. Throat of a stickleback, is it not enough to transfix the song sparrow with your verse? Of all the smoky sou'westers I ever seen, we are having the beatermost. The sun looks like a round ball of fire, and White Island and Duck are entirely hidden in smoke. Chicago, Wisconsin, and Michigan burning up. Mother thinks to start very soon. Bocky hates to have her go and thinks she will not be able to come back till spring. Lucy is on the war-path. Caroline rolls up her eyes and says her stay on this terrestrial sphere will be short indeed. I hope you are getting along well. All are well at the island and send loads of love.

Most affectionately,
Cedy

* * *October 30, 1871* * *

Dear Sister,

. . . We are delighted to hear that you are going to have the poems published all together. We can sell four million copies in our shop, if you don't object. . . . The time of Mother's starting is very uncertain. There is a good deal of work to be done yet, and she dislikes to leave while Amos is here. Caroline says she will not stay with Lucy and wants desperately to get on the county farm again, up in Brentwood. She is the most unfortunate person I ever saw, and she is awful hard to manage. Lucy went over to Inglebritzens' last eve. and stayed till ½ past 9 o'clock. Today we found out that two gallant Norwegians (not of Inglebrit family, however) fought for the honor of escorting the fair creature home, and were pounded awful. One went in to Ports. this morning early to get a sheriff to take the other one to jail. And thus we while away our hours. All send loads of love to all.

Most sincerely and lovingly,
Cedy

*   *   *November 23, 1871*   *   *

Dear Sister,

. . . We have received two nice letters from you since I last wrote, and also the novel *Guilt and Innocence,* for which you have our thanks. We were glad to learn by your last letter that you were not entirely carried away by the terrific storm. *We* came very near a watery grave, here at the island, for the sea was terrific—far beyond anything of the kind experienced in this vicinity for the last twenty years. The waves came up over the boardwalk that extends from the house to the shore, and carried away a part of the "slip"; made mince meat of our bathing platform, and did lots of mischief. Bocky and Pip were out in it all day with the only two suits of rubbers. The *Lone Star* was in the upper dock, and the number of lines that they put out to her was perfectly astonishing. Bocky came up in a breathing space to the piazza, where I was; and after regarding her for a few seconds contemplatively, said in a whisper, "I didn't know there was so much rigging in the world."

The Inglebrits came over in the midst of the storm and told us of the havoc the sea was making over their way. Every boat on their moorings was carried off or sunk, and Mrs. Inglebrit in the vain endeavor to save her hens came very near sharing the same fate, for a big sea struck the hen-coop in which was Mrs. I. and filled it with water and knocked it from its foundation. The story is that Mrs. Inglebrit jumped sixty feet through the open door of the coop into the open arms of her son Julius, and was carried fainting into the residence above.

The day after the storm, Bocky picked up an iron can buoy,

such as they use in harbors. It was passing by, close by the western shore, at the rate of forty knots an hour just as the sun rose. Bocky saw it from his window and caught it by Halfway Rock. We had a hard pull to get it home, but it is a valuable prize.

The breakers ("The splendid breakers, how they rush tumultuous up the rocky slope")[1] in Broad Cove were magnificent. I wish you had been here to see. . . . Caroline has behaved so well lately that we are all frightened. She actually begins to see the bright side of things. Mother thinks to start the first *real* pleasant day now, but I think it will be some time yet before she gets started.

There isn't much news. I will write you more particulars of the storm soon if I don't see you first. All send loads of love.

Most aff.,
Cedy

1. "The splendid breakers, etc.": Adapted from Celia's poem "The Minute Guns." The second stanza reads:
> The splendid breakers! How they rushed,
>   All emerald green and flashing white,
> Tumultuous in the morning sun,
>   With cheer and sparkle and delight!

* * *December 3, 1871* * *

Dear Sister,

. . . We like "Boon Island Watch" very much. Is it to be published in the book with the others? The Inglebrits are getting along nicely again, and are getting new gear as fast as possible. Mother was glad to hear that the box pleased you. I have eat thousands and thousands of Thanksgiving dinners, but I never eat such a nice Thanksgiving dinner as we had the other day. We all wished for you so much. Pip has been off for a week and so Mother has not felt like starting and leaving Bocky all alone, Amos being gone, you know. If the weather is pleasant, she will start as soon as Pip gets back. But I imagine it will be the middle of the month before she gets started. . . .

They have had considerable sickness at Star Island this fall. The whole of William Robinson's family have had the typhoid fever. Albert, the youngest boy, died two or three days ago. They borrowed the *Lone Star* to get the coffin. He was quite a nice little fellow and about fifteen years old.

Caroline is getting quite didactic. She talks so learnedly that we are quite in the shade and ready to hide our diminished heads. I'm afraid she will crush Bocky into the earth when Mother and I are gone. . . . I hope soon to jump out of a carriage at Newtonville and heave Mother slap into your face.

Aff.,
Cedy

* * *December 7, 1871* * *

Dear Sister,

. . . We have had a most tremendous spell of weather at the islands. It has been very cold, and it blows continually. . . . If we didn't keep a good supply of hot rocks, I don't know what would become of us. Today has been rather more moderate. This forenoon Sammy Robinson came over after milk, and gave Mother some of the current gossip of Gosport, which kept her in a roar of laughter for *tew* hours. In the afternoon Brooks came over with a firkin of fat mackerel from Lem and three big dunfish from Origen. . . . How many Norwegians dew yew suppose there are in the small house on the foreside? . . . There are sixteen! You know the house, and so I ask yew where in under the light of the sun they stow themselves? It must be somewhat after the manner of sandwiches. . . .

Pip has not come back yet. We expect him every day. Mother and I will start (it's getting rather old, I know) the first chance after Pip gets back. Bocky is dearer than tongue can tell. All send loads of love to all.

Aff.,
Cedy

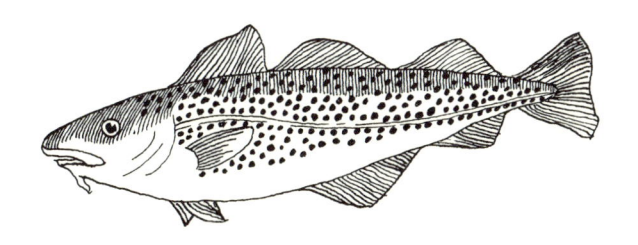

* * *December 14, 1871* * *

Dear Gwammy,

... Mother uses such big words nowadays that Bocky and I have to carry dictionaries slung around our necks. She said yesterday evening, as she gazed at the eastern sky flushed by the last rays of the setting sun, "Oh! Do see how *lumerous* those clouds are!" Bocky and I are crushed into the earth with big words. We don't know which way to turn or where to go. Pip has not got back yet. Mother says tell Sister that just as soon as Pip gets back and a pleasant day comes (it's getting very, very old, I know) we shall start. Pip started to shingle his mother's house and said he would be gone three days, and it is now nearly three weeks since he departed. I hate to go off and leave Bocky to the tender mercies of Lucy and Caroline. I'm afraid he will starve to death, for the plain facts are that Lucy is a careless, slipshod girl, and Cal is beyond talk. But it may stir him up into getting a wife, which would be the best thing for him, in my opinion. ...

Most aff.,
Cedy

* * *January 4, 1872* * *

Dear Gwammy,

Well, if it is a merry happy new year, why in under the light of the sun don't you say so? Thank you, dear; so glad. Your little book came in time for a happy new year's present. The poems are perfect gems, every one, and "Land-locked" brought the tears into your beauty mother's eyes, straightway. To think that Miss Cushman is going to read "Boon Island Watch" in public. If you go to hear it, you must be sure to tell us how you like hearing your own poems read. How many copies of your book in the edition? You speak as if there were but 500, and as Mr. T. pays $500 for publishing, it puzzles me to tell where the profit is coming in at a dollar a copy. But perhaps it is the next edition. Can't you tell us? Well, why can't ye? ...

Bocky and Pip and I work in the shop in cold weather. We are making nicknacks to sell in the shop. I occasionally take my gun and rush round the island after a loon or a seal, and thus while away an hour. I wish you could have been here to supper the other evening to have stood up and set down and laughed with us. Caroline, looking over the almanac, said, "Half your corn and half your hay, I wonder when it is *Scandalmuss Day.*" That made Pip laugh so that he came near choking, and Bocky rushed at him with the tea-kettle full of boiling water and stood over him in an attitude to strike terror to the young soul. And then the kitchen was in an uproar, of course. John Cook is quite sick—not expected to live. Hewes, the minister, says it is the effect of drink. Mother and I expect to start, the first chance, for the continent. And thus we while away our hours.

> With much love,
> Cedy

* * *January 5, 1872* * *

Dear Gwammy,

John Cook is dead. I write this small note to tell you, as he used to be a friend of Mr. T's. He died early this morning, and John Caswell came over after breakfast to get Bocky to make a coffin. Poor Bocky didn't relish the job, but he complied with the grace of a Christian. If you will believe me, John Caswell was miserably drunk, and on such an errand, too. It was dreadful, but Bocky and I could not help laughing at his grotesque contortions. I suppose he would have *sung* if we had asked him. I rather think John Cook died miserably poor. Mother is beauty, and is going to start the first chance. I'm afraid we are going to lose the Inglebrits, as they desire to hire a privilege at Smutty (Johnson's lease being up). John Huntress[1] has already hired one house at Smutty and also Ols Christian Polson. (I write the name in full with pride at having mastered it.) G. A. Emery[2] is writing a book about the Shoals. I hope he will spare you. With much love to all.

> Aff.,
> Cedy

1. John Huntress: This is probably John Hontvet, as renamed by the Shoalers. The following year his family was victimized by Louis Wagner in the famous Smuttynose murders. See the note on Karen Christensen, p. 160.

2. George Alexander Emery was known regionally as both historian and typographer. Cedric apparently refers here to *Ancient and Modern Isles of Shoals,* which Emery published in 1872 but which was written by M. Tzl. Montegeu.

* * March 8, 1872 * *

Dear Sister,

. . . Such a cold spell has not been experienced in these parts for fifteen years. The white owl for all his feathers was acold and has betaken himself on downy pinions to a milder clime. The icebergs in the coves on the west side of the island are tremendous, and all the shore is covered with a heavy coating of glittering ice. The therm. last Tuesday morning indicated six degrees below zero, and it didn't get above all day.

Pip went to Ports. last Monday with Inglebritzen and didn't get back till today (Friday). He tells a wonderful story about people walking across the Piscataqua from New Castle to Kittery, and how the vessels, including the *Lone Star,* had to be cut out of the ice &c., &c., but we told him it was all a d——d lie and we didn't believe a word of it, and that we had been at work every day in our shirt sleeves and had to keep putting snow and ice on our heads to prevent sunstroke. Pip's eyes stuck out a few feet, but we "cussed" him up hill and down dale, so he got no chance to contradict us.

The flowers are all safe, though two leaves and a bud froze on the lily, and we could have cried about it if it would have done any good. Pip brought your good letter of March 6, and we are very glad to hear Mother is getting along so nicely. She is one beauty, and she mustn't worry about us or anything. We are doing nobly. Lucy contrives to cook us quite a variety, and altogether does much better than I expected. Our principal dish is "pate de foi gras"!!! We haven't got any mason yet. They will not come till after election, anyway, and if we *had* got one, the weather has been too cold to do anything.

Rumors of the strife and warfare of election begin to circulate in the land. Lemmy and Elvin are the rival candidates for representative at Gosport, and I expect the meeting house will be knocked flat by the hardy voters. Elvin has been buying votes; rumor says, ten votes at $30.00 a vote. And then he is making presents to the voters' wives, and in fact using every means, fair or foul, to secure election. Lemmy, meanwhile, is tearing round the island like a maniac, threatening to scalp every man, woman, and child that crosses his path. . . .

       Aff.,
       Cedy

*   *   *March 15, 1872*   *   *

Dear Sister,

Yours of the 10th was received yesterday, and a more shorter or more horrider letter it has never been our misfortune to receive. Is there nothing happening in your *vy*cinity worthy of the name of news? . . . And then you hardly mentioned that dear mother! I suppose because you have got her you think you are all right, and never mind if we starve. Pretty soon, howsomever, we will come and get her away from you if we can ketch her, and then you will write us longer letters.

Well, things are going on pretty well here. The plasterer, Bob Lock, came yesterday, and he has got the kitchen nearly plastered. I guess he will finish everything by next Wednesday. Then Bocky will start for Boston and Pip and I will paint the pastry-room so as to have it ready when that beauty mother gets home. As Bocky will remain in Boston ten days or a fortnight, perhaps she will come back with him.

The town meeting at Gosport turned out a complete failure, for Ephraim Henry,[1] Duckshooter and chief *see*lectman, refused to have anything to do with it; and notwithstanding the curses of Elvin and the tears of Lemmy, the whole thing resulted in a mizzle. The next day, however, Elvin took his whole company of voters up to the watch house in Ports., and obtained the services of the City Marshal and twenty-five policemen, two state constables, and a N. Y. detective, and meandered forth in search of the aforesaid *see*lectman who broke up the meeting. The *see*lectman, however, used to many feints and much cunning in his vocation of Duckshooter, succeeded in putting himself beyond the strong arm of the law. Lemmy says that Hatch says that it is a clear case of "nilly pro con," and that the law must take its course; while Elvin, who has expended nigh ontew a thousand dollars, with the hope of going to the Legislature, swears to have the blood of every *see*lectman on Star Island ere another slender crescent shines again. Thus stands the election at Gosport, but in the state it has gone entirely Repub., as, I suppose, you must be aware.

Lucy has had a fearful toothache, but she is all right now. It lasted four days, and during that time she and Caroline drank a half a barrel of gin and two doz. bts. pine. . . .

With lots of love to all, and a hug for that dear Mother,

Most aff:.,
O. & C.

1. Ephraim Henry: E. H. Downs, born in 1840, son of John Bragg Downs.

* * *April 15, 1872* * *

Dear Sister,

I should have answered your two good letters before this, but my good right hand has been maimed so I could not grip a pen in a satisfactory manner. While helping raise the gas house last Sat. I fell sixty feet in the perpendicular and rebounded some two hundred and nine feet in the clear, striking upon the aforesaid hand with desultory results. I thank you for the photo, and think you are one beauty. Mother is getting along first rate, and didn't take any cold coming out. . . . She is making lots of new dresses, with Miss Tobey's help, and they look beauty.

The gas pipers came and commenced business last Saturday. There are two of them, and they think it will take six weeks to finish. The men with the gas machine are coming very soon. We are very busy getting things ready. Bocky works as usual, like a steam engine. The gas house is quite a stylish building, being twenty feet high and six sided, and we are going to put on an ornamental finish and paint and so forth. . . .

Affectionately and in haste,
Cedy

* * *May 5, 1872* *

Dear Sister,

. . . I wish you could see Mother's flowers; they flourish beyond talk, and blaze with blossoms and beauty. And no tongue can tell how she enjoys them. She keeps saying, "I think they beat Sister's." We have been waging war against the dirt and dust for the past week. You see the gas fitters have to take the carpets partly up in every room, and I have to follow on and make repairs. In some rooms I find the mattress under the carpet, the spring in the ventilator, knots tied in the bolster, and the bureau through the mosquito bar. Thus we while away our hours.

I cleaned out the help's rooms the other day, got a barrel of dirt and dust, and found 2 blankets, 12 napkins, 8 towels, 4 sheets, and 10 pillow-slips beneath the attic floor. Some poor girl had gone off forgetting to steal them. I sympathize with her deeply. . . .

Most aff.,
Cedy

* * *June 9, 1872* *

Dear Sister,

. . . Well, the gas has been tried and is very successful. The light is magnificent, and makes the whole establishment very brilliant in the evening. We have got a big burner in a lantern right at the head of the slip for Sat. nights and late parties. It lights the slip and surroundings wonderfully. We only anticipate one trouble, and that is that the holder or gasometer is rather small. It holds, however, 1600 feet, and all the burners are one foot (foot of gas per hour), so hope it will be big enough.

We have got the *Ada* & *Pilgrim* off, and two whale boats, and it begins to look lively. Mr. Tiffany, engineer of gas operations, is here with his wife and son. Mrs. T. seems to be a lovely woman, and admires your poetry. Yesterday Pip fell off of the gasometer, a distance of ten feet, striking his hip on a barrel of oil and his head on the ledge. When Bocky and I got to him, the blood was flowing from a wound in his head, and he was white as a sheet. Today he is better, however, though he hobbles about in a dismal manner. . . .

We are having rather bad luck with our live stock. Black Bess is most dead, and the cow we bought last summer is in the same plight; and last night we lost a beautiful heifer calf 5 months old. The late storm tore up a part of the slip which we had just got fixed. Such is life. Lucy is soon to go to Boston for a week, and is going to come out to your house to stay all night. Mother wanted me to tell you, so you could let her stay with Hannah.

All send loads of love.

Most aff.,
Cedy

*   *   *February 9, 1873*   *   *

Dear Sister,

You are a beauty critter. I believe I acknowledged yours of the 4th in my last short note. Mother was very much pleased to get the photograph of Longfellow. She was telling Caroline about it, and says Cal, "Who is Longfellow? Never heard of him before." Mother held up her hands with astonishment depicted on every lineament of her countenance. It *is* terrible to contemplate, isn't it? I have been reading *Cyrilla* lately, and find it very interesting. What a time you must be having with the *Shoals*. Have you written much additional?

We have got all the things out that Bocky bought at the Waverley House. There is a centrifugal wringer that cost new, five hundred dollars, and a steam table that cost still more. Then there are two washing machines of the most approved make, the apparatus for a steam drying room, eight jacketed kettles that cost when new a hundred dollars apiece, a large range and broiler, a mangle, eight soapstone wash tubs, a large oak table for meat cook, a large sink partitioned for washing dishes, a brick oven, and various other small things. He got the whole for a thousand dollars!!!

Spitz has gone to New Castle. Push[1] was out for a day or two, and we took the opportunity to get rid of him. Flapps has been banished to the big kitchen, where he plays with the big Newfoundland dog as he used to with Spitz.

Nearly all the Gosportians left have been over here lately, and they one and all say(?) that they bitterly regret having sold their homesteads.[2] They are all down on Mathes to the lowest notch. Lem was up in Mother's room talking to her for two hours, and she did nothing but laugh! Lem says if he don't get a place on the Shoals to live, he shall be crazy. John Bragg[3] has received offers for houselots from all the Shoalers who emigrated to Portsmouth in the fall.

The new building at Star is beginning to make quite a show. They have got nearly all the frame up. It extends from the Newton place to the fish houses by the Ram's Horn, two hundred & sixty feet. They expect to expend $350,000 before they get ready.

Mother's flowers begin to look greener and more flourishing. They feel that spring is coming. The days are an hour and a quarter longer; isn't that good? We are getting along slowly with our work. Amos has left us for his periodical drunk. The painters are *fearfully* slow, but they may get through by the time boarders arrive. Pip has been so sick that he has been unable to work for a week. Mother has entirely recovered from her cold.

All send love.

Aff.,
Cedy

1. Push: "Push of New Castle was barber and keeper of store for many years." (Handwritten note on corner of letter.)
2. having sold their homesteads: John R. Poor of Somerville, Mass., a partner in the spice and mustard firm of Stickney and Poor, was a guest at

Appledore in the summer of 1872. Through an agent, Nathan F. Mathes of Portsmouth, he succeeded in buying out all but two of the Gosport residents, in preparation for establishing a large hotel on Star Island. He did not preserve his anonymity long, for the Portsmouth *Daily Chronicle* announced on September 2 that "Mr. Poore [*sic*] . . . is the gentleman who has purchased Star Island." However, the Gosportians who later regretted their action aimed their resentment at Mathes, the man who had dealt with them directly.

Two items of interest appeared in the Portsmouth *Evening Times* of September 10 and 13:

> We are promised that we shall soon have full details of the proposed improvement on Star Island. It is said that there are quite a number of capitalists who would be glad to take stock in the enterprise. The report that Messrs. Laighton of the Appledore are opposed to it, is not true. There is business enough for all and there will never be hotels enough built on the Isles of Shoals to accommodate all who wish to rest there during the months of July and August. (Sept. 10, 1872)

> The Sale of Star Island, and Proposed Improvements.—Mr. N. F. Mathes of this city having purchased the land of all the owners of Star Island at the Isles of Shoals, except two on the southerly side who will retain their homes, a town meeting was held on Thursday to see what action the town of Gosport would take in regard to the common lands owned by the town. All parties seemed anxious to close up the whole matter and a unanimous vote was passed authorizing the selectmen to give to Mr. Mathes a deed of all the land of the town, in consideration that he would assume and pay so much of the war debt and the taxes of the years 1871 and 1872 as is equal to the proportion that the individuals who have sold their land to him would be called upon to pay, amounting to thirty-eight hundred dollars. The deed is to be given immediately and the money paid into the town treasury. Mr. Mathes thus becomes the owner of the whole of Star Island, excepting a small portion which is not in the way of the proposed improvements.

> It is intended to move back all the houses on the Island that are worth saving for cottages, and level off and grade the whole front down to the water. A wharf will be built of stone, at which the largest steamer can land its passengers from the deck. A large hotel will be erected as soon as possible, with all modern appliances necessary for a first class watering place. All of the business has thus far been transacted in the name of Mr. Mathes alone, although it is understood that Boston capitalists are associated with him. (Sept. 13, 1872)

3. John Bragg: *I.e.*, John Bragg Downs. He and Rev. George Beebe were the two holdouts. Beebe had retired from the ministry of the church in 1869 and moved from the parsonage, but continued his residence on the Island.

*   *   *February 23, 1873*   *   *

Dear Sister,

. . . You must know that Caroline has had an awful "spell," not very long, as it has lasted but three days, but for intensity hardly equaled by the earthquake at St. Thomas. The first day was a fearful day, and will long be remembered in the annals of Appledore, for on that day Caroline stalked into the pastry-room at ten o'clock, took her accustomed seat in the rocking chair on the weather side of the stove, just abaft the teakettle, placed her chin upon her extended right hand, rocked gently back and forth, gazed abstractedly into the oven, and burst out into some of the most fearfully dismal and piercingly heartrending yells I ever heard. The very windows shuddered in their casements, and the horses, up at the barn, catching the sound as it eddied round on the wings of the northwester, lifted their heads and snorted and tugged at their fastenings in deadly fear. The cows moved uneasily in their stalls, and the lowing herd wound slowly o'er the lea. . . .

You well may guess that Mother was neither pleased nor edified by this exhibition, and she did everything she could think of to stop the flood of misery—but unavailingly. As well might you try to stem the current of the swift Piscataqua, or row up the falls of Niagara! At last, baffled and beaten, worn and worried beyond endurance, Mother bethought her of hiding the spectacle from sight, and forthwith erected a barricade of chairs and shawls; and when Bocky and I came in to dinner, there was the beleaguered fortress Caroline, dimly visible through the canopy of chairs and shawls, with her chin still in her hand and wailing like the stormy northeaster off the coast of Labrador. Since that fearful experience she has been steadily improving, and today she has been talking of the recent deaths at Newington in an almost cheerful manner.

The cause of this "spell" was the departure of Karen Christensen,[1] of which event I will now proceed to give you a detailed account. The sleeping apartments occupied by the workmen connected with the Appledorean mansion had not been washed and hardly swept since October's lunar crescent shone o'er the encircling seas. This coming under Mother's observation, she directed Karen to sweep and wash them after the manner of Capt. John Smith, who killed Pocahontas, you know (or don't you know). Well, you should have seen the righteous indignation of Karen as she stood in Mother's doorway, clutching the doorknob in her feverish grasp and with the fire of her pent up emotions flashing from either eye. Well, enough to say that she annihilated Mother; fairly crushed her into the earth and departed from the room in a perfect whirlwind of broken English, Northern and Southern Norwegian, Sanskrit, and High Dutch, from which I picked out passages evidently quoted from the battle of King Olaf with Svend the Dane, wherein a bowman says to Olaf, "That was Norway slipping from thy hand, O King!" The next day she expressed sorrow, but Mother was fairly aroused, and she gave her money and said, "Depart, and never come in my sight again." So she departed, and Caroline, thinking it was done to spite her, subsided into the melancholy condition I have described. . . .

Lemmy has got the law ontew Poor & Mathes, and Hackett has got the case. Poor & Mathes are getting along well with the new hotel at Star. It is up and boarded but not roofed yet, and the place begins to look quite gay. Lucy and Pip are more loving than ever. Thora[2] sings a song that our old music box used to play, and is a very good girl generally. The other day I rowed away off to the southeast six or eight miles after meowls. The ocean was perfectly calm and the air was mild and pleasant. Meowls and large gulls flew over my boat in large numbers, and I shot fifteen. I rowed by a vessel and saw five or six men on deck busily baiting a trawl. They told me in some alarm that my shot struck their vessel. I apologized and rowed away, leaving them in the dead calm with their sails flapping against the mast and the skipper sitting dejectedly upon the tiller. . . . It is some time since we heard from you, but the *Lone Star* is now in Portsmouth, and we are looking forward to a letter from you which will tell us when to expect you in Ports. All send loads of love.

Most aff.,
Cedy

1. Karen Christensen: Celia, who wrote several poems on her Norwegian neighbors, begins her poem "Karen" as follows:

> At her low quaint wheel she sits to spin,
> > Deftly drawing the long, light rolls
> Of carded wool through her fingers thin,
> > By the fireside by the Isles of Shoals.
>
> She is not pretty, she is not young,
> > Poor homesick Karen, who sits and spins,
> Humming a song in her native tongue,
> > That falters and stops, and again begins,
>
> While her wheel flies fast, with its drowsy hum,
> > And she makes a picture of pensive grace
> As the thoughts of her well-loved Norway come
> > And deepen the shadows across her face. . . .

But Karen was to have a greater claim to fame. She was one of the two victims of the notorious murderer Louis Wagner on March 6, 1873, less than a fortnight after Cedric wrote this letter. For details of that gruesome event, read *Moonlight Murder at Smuttynose* by Lyman V. Rutledge, or his briefer account in *The Isles of Shoals in Lore and Legend*.

2. Thora: One of the young Ingebretsons and the subject of another of Celia's poems. Thora was called "Tooler" by the Gosportians.

* * *October 10, 1875* * *

Dear Sister,

I hardly know where to direct this letter. Mayhap you are in Montpelier, and then again you may be in New York, Chicago, or the Thuringian Forest; for judging from your letters you must be continually on the move from one part of our country to the other. We [are] all constantly expecting to see your name booked aboard a Cunarder for distant Europe, Asia, and the Isle of Man.

Mother is first rate. She sleeps all night and is free from aches and pains, though she dreads the thoughts of the cold winter to come.

The Ingebertsens, having purchased Preble's Island in the river at Portsmouth, are moving off, and Pip and Lucy are going to take the house.

We haven't had the mail for nearly a week. Hope to get it today. Oscar hasn't been very well for a week past. No news to write about. I'm growing fat, weigh 210 lbs. My consolation is that you outweigh me.

All send love.

Most affectionately,
Cedy

* * * October 20, 1875 * *

Dear Sister,

We received three or four letters from you from Vermont. I suppose now you are in California, but I'm going to send this to Newtonville and risk it. Mother says you are a beautycritter to write her such nice long letters, and we all think it is charming to read of the manners and customs of all the different places in the world. But we cannot and will not believe that the Montpelier coffee is better than ours. Throat of a stickleback! it cannot be. Oh, the fresh fish chowders that we are having, and the cods' heads and tongues, and preserved haddocks' eyes, and scalloped fins, and lobster shortcake, and one stuff or another. The fabled goodies of Vermont State sink into the merest twaddle, when compared with the delicacies under which our table groans. But there, dear, you cannot have everything in this world. And then you vaunt the beauties of the Vermont woods. "They may be red, but air they too red?" If you appreciate that sort of thing, you should be here to see the airs our elm tree puts on ere it throws its naked arms to the northwesters. Green and gold, a thousand thousand prismatic hues are struggling with the ten leaves, till the eye is overcome with the radiance. And then the huckleberry bushes upon the hill!!! Oh my goodness, if you could only see um. Layer upon layer of scarlet corn color, and velvet maroon green, with here and there the soft grey of the rocks gleaming between; with the brilliant plumage of the song sparrow flashing like a piece of lemon peel on a rum punch, and the melodious cry of the sea gull mixed all up in amongst it. This is a picture that one never forgets.

Mother's flowers are thriving at a great rate. All the geraniums are in bloom. . . . The weather here is beautiful.

Yours ever affectionately,
Cedy

AFTERWORD

The letters end here, except for a scattered few in later years. Celia was now spending more time at the Islands, and was learning the news at first hand. For our purposes, this is a good stopping place, for the letters have carried us to a turning point in Shoals history.

Poor's new hotel, the Oceanic, enjoyed two good seasons in 1873 and 1874; then burned to the ground. Still hopeful for the future, Poor moved to a new site, connecting the old Gosport and Atlantic Houses with a new structure between them, and attaching the John Caswell residence to the rear. Using several of the older buildings for additional sleeping space, he was able to house two hundred and fifty guests. But after one season with the new Oceanic, he changed his mind and sold out to the Laighton Brothers. Thus, in the spring of 1876, Oscar and Cedric became indeed the lords of the Isles. That same year Gosport held its last town meeting and was officially annexed to Rye; thereby ending two and a half centuries of year-round community life.

But Celia, Oscar, and Cedric were still young, and much living lay ahead.

REFERENCES

Adams, Charles Francis. *Richard Henry Dana.* 2 vols. Boston and New York: Houghton, Mifflin, 1891.

Downs, John W. *Sprays of Salt.* Privately printed, 1944.

"Gosport Town Records," *New England Historical and Genealogical Register,* LXVII-LXVIII (Jan. 1913-Apr. 1914).

Howe, M. A. DeWolfe. *Memories of a Hostess.* Boston: Atlantic Monthly Press, 1922.

Laighton, Oscar. *Ninety Years at the Isles of Shoals.* Andover, Mass.: Andover Press, 1929.

Portsmouth *Chronicle*: Jan. 12, 1865; Sept. 11, 1865; Mar. 25, 1868; Feb. 27, 1871; Sept. 2, 1872.

Portsmouth *Evening Times*: Sept. 10, 1872; Sept. 13, 1872.

Rutledge, Lyman V. *The Isles of Shoals in Lore and Legend.* Barre, Mass.: Barre Press, 1965.

Rutledge, Lyman V. *The Isles of Shoals in Lore and Legend.* Omnibus Edition. 6 vols., typescript. 1965.

Society for Propagating the Gospel among the Indians and Others in North America. Annual Reports.

Thaxter, Celia. *Among the Isles of Shoals.* Boston: James R. Osgood, 1873.

Thaxter, Celia. *Poems.* New York: Hurd and Houghton, 1872.

Thaxter, Rosamond. *Sandpiper: The Life of Celia Thaxter.* Sanbornville, N. H.: Wake-Brook House, 1962.